Praise for *Manifest Momen.*

"I am in awe of the clarity these women bring to such a potentially transforming mission. To simplify access to the world's mysteries we ourselves house is by far the most sophisticated task in the world, and to achieve this you don't have to be a member of any clan—you can just enter with this book."

— **Charlotte Beers**, CEO, Chairman,
Undersecretary of State, and Teacher

*"If you are a high achiever who is interested in experiencing success without struggle and strain, this book will show you the pathway. **Manifest Moment to Moment** is now my new favorite book on listening to, trusting, and acting on my intuition. I love that I can take it in tiny bite-size pieces as my busy schedule allows and experience the <u>huge</u> results that come from the subtle, gentle shifts in my awareness. This book nourishes my own self-understanding and gives me the courage to go deeper."*

— **Baeth Davis**, Innovative Purpose Mentor and
The Palm Pilot for the Soul of Your Business™

*"Within each of us runs a deep river of truth—a wide body of wisdom desiring to know itself, longing to manifest into relevant expressions of service to human evolution and ultimate freedom of the soul. Our lives can carry this interior wisdom from soul to body . . . from inspiration to manifestation. How? **Manifest Moment to Moment** takes on this question. Rather than finding a way <u>to</u> this truth, Tejpal and Dr. Carrol McLaughlin encourage you to find your way <u>out</u> of all the ways in which you are stuck. Unstuck, the truth becomes self-revealing . . . manifesting moment to moment!"*

— **Deborah Jones**, Executive Director,
Nine Gates Programs, Inc.

*"**Manifest Moment to Moment** conveys with authenticity a practice that, when one uses intuition and understands the energy of the chakras, can elevate your journey and seemingly bring magic to life. Tejpal and Dr. Carrol's thoughtful writing provides the ultimate mindfulness for personal well-being!"*

— **Michael Tompkins**, Chief Executive Officer,
Miraval Resort & Spa

MANIFEST

MOMENT TO MOMENT

ALSO BY DR. CARROL MCLAUGHLIN

DR. CARROL'S POWER PERFORMANCE

HAY HOUSE TITLES OF RELATED INTEREST

YOU CAN HEAL YOUR LIFE, the movie,
starring Louise Hay & Friends
(available as a 1-DVD program and an expanded 2-DVD set)
Watch the trailer at: www.LouiseHayMovie.com

THE SHIFT, the movie,
starring Dr. Wayne W. Dyer
(available as a 1-DVD program and an expanded 2-DVD set)
Watch the trailer at: www.DyerMovie.com

MANIFEST YOUR DESIRES:
365 Ways to Make Your Dreams a Reality,
by Esther and Jerry Hicks (the Teachings of Abraham®)

MINDFUL LIVING, by Miraval

THE POWER IS WITHIN YOU, by Louise Hay

SOUL COACHING®: 28 Days to Discover Your Authentic Self,
by Denise Linn

TUNE IN: Let Your Intuition Guide You to Fulfillment and Flow,
by Sonia Choquette

WISHES FULFILLED: Mastering the Art of Manifesting,
by Dr. Wayne W. Dyer

All of the above are available at your
local bookstore, or may be ordered by visiting:

Hay House USA: www.hayhouse.com®
Hay House Australia: www.hayhouse.com.au
Hay House UK: www.hayhouse.co.uk
Hay House South Africa: www.hayhouse.co.za
Hay House India: www.hayhouse.co.in

MANIFEST
MOMENT TO MOMENT

8 Principles to Create the Life You Truly Desire

TEJPAL and
DR. CARROL McLAUGHLIN

HAY HOUSE, INC.
Carlsbad, California • New York City
London • Sydney • Johannesburg
Vancouver • Hong Kong • New Delhi

Published and distributed in the United States by: Hay House, Inc.: www .hayhouse.com® • **Published and distributed in Australia by:** Hay House Australia Pty. Ltd.: www.hayhouse.com.au • **Published and distributed in the United Kingdom by:** Hay House UK, Ltd.: www.hayhouse.co.uk • **Published and distributed in the Republic of South Africa by:** Hay House SA (Pty), Ltd.: www.hayhouse.co.za • **Distributed in Canada by:** Raincoast Books: www.raincoast.com • **Published in India by:** Hay House Publishers India: www.hayhouse.co.in

Cover and interior design: Tricia Breidenthal

Illustration on page 131 © Christie McMearty. Used by permission.

The Process for Self-Discovery exercise in Chapter 8 was developed by Dr. Ann Marie Chiasson and reprinted with permission.

Library of Congress Cataloging-in-Publication Data

Tejpal.
 Manifest moment to moment : 8 principles to create the life you truly desire / Tejpal and Dr. Carrol McLaughlin.
    pages cm
 ISBN 978-1-4019-4182-6 (tradepaper : alk. paper) 1. Self-realization. 2. Conduct of life. 3. Spiritual life. I. McLaughlin, Carrol. II. Title.
 BJ1470.T43 2014
 158--dc23
                                                2013042354

Tradepaper ISBN: 978-1-4019-4182-6

17 16 15 14   4 3 2 1
1st edition, June 2014

SUSTAINABLE FORESTRY INITIATIVE
Certified Chain of Custody
Promoting Sustainable Forestry
www.sfiprogram.org
SFI-01268

SFI label applies to the text stock

Printed in the United States of America

CONTENTS

PREFACE

....

On Meeting Each Other

Tejpal: It was a Monday night, and I was playing guitar at a Kundalini yoga class in Tucson, Arizona. At the end of the class, a vivacious blonde woman came to the stage and complimented me on my playing. She said she was a harpist and invited me to play music with her sometime. I was struck by the life force and joy in her eyes, and I saw a very clear message in my mind that we would do creative work together.

Carrol: I remember always running from teaching my university class to taking a yoga class every Monday night. Always a little bit late, I'd change quickly into yoga pants and take a deep breath as I slid at the last second onto my yoga mat. Most of the classes have blurred into one memory, except for the evening that Tejpal touched my soul with her music and ability to connect so deeply with others. I was mesmerized by the power and depth of wisdom that surrounded Tejpal and emanated from her. I remember knowing immediately that I wanted to perform with her. Since I was headed to Brazil for a concert tour, we decided to meet and play some music together at my house after I returned.

On Working Together

Tejpal: A few weeks later when Carrol opened the door, I saw her golden harp on display in her front room. As we started to play and compose together, it was as if we had done so for years. I was filled with joy.

As I got to know Carrol, I was impressed by her incredible creativity in every area of her life. She approaches everything from the belief "of course you can" and is able to infuse this energy into everyone she comes in contact with. Her focus and the power of her determination continually amaze me. Her vitality, joy, and ability to uplift are a priceless gift to everyone she meets. I often laugh at how successfully she does so many things and wonder how one human being can manifest so much in one lifetime.

As we spent more time together, we shared our beliefs and ambitions, and we discovered that we had a common soul longing to inspire and uplift others. We realized that although our life experiences were in different areas, the mission behind our actions was the same. We both felt an extraordinarily strong desire to help others discover how to tap into and express their fullest potential.

This shared passion to empower others led us to design and teach many workshops together: on intuition, soulful creativity, healing, the human energy field, and maximizing your potential. In addition, we began giving personal and group healing and coaching sessions as a team.

Carrol: Whenever I had the opportunity to work with Tejpal, I always found myself astonished by how she could envelop everyone she met with her mesmerizing energy. She would engage each person and encourage him or her to go deep within—being direct, provocative, funny, and nurturing all at the same time. I am in awe of the power of her presence and her facility in changing lives. The true joy and deep respect we have for each other creates a unique spirit wherever we go.

I remember one instance in Cairo, Egypt, where we gave a Personal Excellence workshop at the Supreme Council of Culture.

The room was filled with a wide variety of people of many ages: intrigued, curious, and motivated to experience new ways of being and manifesting what they desired in their lives. The enthusiasm in the room was contagious, and Tejpal and I were both extremely grateful for this opportunity to assist people as they opened up to new possibilities. Our combined energy seemed to be a win-win for everyone, and we could feel the magic in the room.

On Writing This Book

Carrol: Driven by our joy in the co-creative process, it soon became very clear to us that we needed to write a book. We wanted to share the successful tools and processes that have helped so many people, and by writing together, that joy and fulfillment was magnified many times.

Tejpal: As we started our book, we quickly found our rhythm. Both living in Tucson, we were able to schedule regular times to write together, always in the same room so the ideas and enthusiasm could bounce back and forth. Carrol created the title and, as we worked, the principles and the structure of the book became more and more obvious. Throughout the several years of writing, wonderful opportunities and people were continually attracted to our project, always exactly the person we needed at the given time to facilitate its growth.

We believe that personal transformation must come from within and cannot be the result of one prescribed formula. Our intent is that you listen to your deepest desires, without preconceived ideas or judgments. Trust the process and, moment to moment, choose the right tool that works for you in your journey toward manifesting the life you truly desire.

INTRODUCTION

If we look at the history of human experience, we discover that there have been numerous periods of extraordinary development. The 18th-century industrial revolution, for example, completely altered the day-to-day reality of many people. Similarly, the age of technology and the accompanying digital revolution of the 1970s deeply affected the world, particularly in 1971 when e-mail was conceived. E-mail, instant texting, personal computers, and telephones with multimedia have changed everyone's relationship with time and made us much more available and accountable for every minute.

With all of this accessibility, the Information Age is overloading humanity with figures and facts. It is easy to become barraged by the constant cacophony of unimportant data and spend much of our time in a reactionary state with little awareness of our thoughts, feelings, and intuition. Whereas the old paradigm was to learn facts and regurgitate them, today there is a mandate to open the mind, be curious, explore, and synthesize the vast knowledge available. Because of the speed with which an idea becomes obsolete, knowledge by itself is no longer perceived as the ultimate truth. The new frontier is to harness the power of personal thought, creativity, and intent, and to cultivate the enormous potential available to us all.

In yogic tradition it is believed that the period of approximately the last 2,000 years, known as the Piscean Age, which was concerned with knowledge, leadership, and increasing expertise, is rapidly coming to a close. The upcoming Aquarian Age necessitates a change in focus toward individual awareness, inner guidance, intuition, and personal wisdom. Today, *these* are the tools for manifesting the life we truly desire, moment to moment, something we were all born to do.

You Are Already a Manifester

Think of those things you have wanted deeply that have manifested in your life. Did you ever desire a job and then hear about the perfect opportunity seemingly "by chance"? Have you always wanted an education and, because of the strength of your desire, made it a reality? Did you need a medical procedure and the doctor you happened to choose was an expert in precisely that field?

You are already a manifester—whether you're aware of it or not. The Merriam-Webster dictionary defines *manifestation* as "a perceptible, outward, or visible expression." If manifestation is an *outward* and *perceptible* expression, then it must have a precursor internally, and thus originate with a thought, a desire, an intent, or a passion.

The exciting part of this phenomenon is that *you* are the agent of manifestation. *You* have the capability and the power to create the life you truly desire—by digging deep inside yourself, discovering the magic of your potential, clearing your limitations, and connecting to your unique soul mission and deepest desires.

Where Manifestation Starts

Everything on the physical plane starts with a vibration, a thought, a desire, or a dream. If your wishes are aligned with who you are and what your soul desire is, they will be fulfilled. When you think of manifestation, there is a tendency to expect something dramatic, a huge change that will magically alter your life. But, in fact, some of the most life-changing manifestations happen on a relatively small level. These seemingly small shifts put you on a new trajectory just one degree over, causing you to arrive at a completely different destination than the course you were previously on. Of course, manifestation can also be so amazing that it takes your breath away, as both of us have experienced.

CARROL'S STORY

In December of 2008, I was overwhelmed, depressed, and worried about my daughter. My whole being was calling out for me to dig out of my malaise, but I didn't seem able to start the journey back to contentment.

I had heard of an inspirational life coach named Joe Vitale. Excited at the idea of having some help and guidance, I contacted his team and learned that he was offering a series of personal coaching sessions. Then, I found out that the price tag for this coaching series was $5,000, an amount that was absolutely impossible for me at that time.

Discouraged, I tried to remain open to possibilities and, on a whim, stopped in to check my mailbox at the University of Arizona, even though we were on Christmas break and there was no reason for me to go there. Inside my mailbox was a solitary envelope, and I opened it with curiosity. In it I found a check for $10,000. It was from a supporter who had come to many of my concerts but whom I did not personally know. All the note said was, "I believe in what you are doing, and this money is to support whatever you need it for."

This generous gift allowed me to work extensively with a life coach, which not only reframed my emotions and my sense of contentment, but also allowed me to manifest and publish my first book, *Power Performance*. I shifted from a place of feeling powerless to being excited about my own potential, and this newfound enthusiasm extended beyond me personally, subsequently inspiring thousands of musicians around the world to believe in themselves and claim their excellence.

TEJPAL'S STORY

Right before Christmas in 1994, I left Paris and moved to New York. I had no support system in the United States, was challenged with a new language, and didn't have a clear picture of what I was going to do.

In Paris I had established a successful career as director of a leadership-development team, but still I felt a longing to experience more joy and self-expression in my life. Intuitively I felt that by following my inner knowing, I would overcome my self-limitations and realize my full potential.

My intuition proved to be correct, because I soon had a very successful executive coaching practice in New York and was experiencing a deeper level of happiness than I had ever known in France.

As you think back over your life, you will find similar occasions when, like Tejpal, you felt the rightness of your path intuitively or when something—like Carrol's unexpected check—occurred to clear the way. You know inherently that manifestation occurs. What you will learn from this book is how to be more intentional and connected to your own essence in that process and how to experience the accompanying awareness and joy. As you work toward manifesting what you desire, as this book encourages and helps you to do, enjoy the journey. Let go of expecting an immediate answer and trust the process.

The Importance of Trust

Wouldn't it be nice in life if you always knew the conclusion before you started? There is a tendency to want to dictate an end result, however impossible that may be. Yet, in life's journey, arrival is a myth. Your story is always unfolding, so a guaranteed ending cannot exist. There can be no single set of instructions for manifesting the life you want, no clear guidelines for your life path. Before figuring out the "how" of your ambition, you must first say "yes" to your desire. When you focus on the "how," you limit yourself by trying to figure out all the steps to make something work. You fast-forward into the future and often create a high level of anxiety.

Instead, honor the incredible power of believing in your dreams, your desires, and your highest aspirations. Carrol's daughter is famous for saying, "If it weren't possible, you wouldn't have thought of it." Trust that what you desire is right for you and can in fact become part of your reality.

We live in an "insurance-based" society. Before you take a risk, you want to know that your "parachute" will catch you. In manifesting moment to moment, you *are* your parachute. Empower your intuition as you learn to rely on your own internal navigation system. Far more powerful than anything you can read or study, the guidance that comes from within you will always serve you. If you follow your true desires, you will experience synchronicity, cooperation, and support. People and opportunities will present themselves just when you need them, and you will find the answers you seek. Trust yourself and have faith. You don't have to be ready—you just have to start!

The Power to Manifest Lies Within You

Because the power to manifest lies in *your* hands, your full participation in this book is essential to create real and lasting shifts in your life. Opportunity for real change is particularly found in the "Claim It!" sections throughout the book. These exercises will lead you through experiences that will have an extraordinary impact on your life. In many of them, you will be writing your responses and feelings. We suggest you set aside a paper journal or space on your favorite digital device—we'll call it your "manifestation journal"—for this work.

Your journey toward manifesting what you desire begins by looking deep inside and uncovering what brings you joy, uplifts you, gives you energy, and makes you unique. This information will serve as a foundation as you design and refine, moment to moment, your extraordinary path toward manifestation. Let's start now with claiming who you truly are!

⊰ Claim It! The Essential Treasure Hunt ⊱

Discover what defines you and what lies at the inner core of your essence. As if you were participating in a child's treasure hunt, allow your imagination to run free. Be playful and relaxed as you write out your answers to the following questions in your manifestation journal.

1. *Values:* What really matters to you? What touches you? What moves you? What do you love? What triggers you and causes you to react?

2. *Personality:* Describe yourself in five words. Some ideas: *quick, lively, bubbly, effervescent, joyful, creative, limitless, caring, colorful, strong, willful, dedicated, committed, compassionate, sensitive, creative, uplifting, naïve, deep, understanding, encouraging, gracious, loving, malleable, funny, honest, direct, complex, clear, simple, basic, practical, esoteric, social, trustworthy.*

3. *Expression*: How do you like to express yourself? For example: painting, playing music, writing, dancing, cooking, gardening, and helping others. How do you think of your communication style: subtle, exuberant, strong, soft-spoken? How do you like to dress? What activities do you like to do? Consider: art, music, charity, sports, coaching, and so on.

4. *Comfort:* When are you at your most peaceful and at ease? Do you like being in a crowd of people, or do you prefer solitude? Does it relax you to read? Write? Exercise? Listen to music?

5. *Yourself and others:* What do you love about yourself? What would you like people to say about you? How do you touch others? What are you proud of?

6. *Joy factor:* If you thought back over several years, what is an action that you took that matters deeply to you? What gives you energy? What uplifts you? What brings you joy?

What did your treasure hunt reveal? Each answer you gave offers a glimpse of your inner core. Like the pieces that compose a stained-glass window, each element is an integral part of the whole picture, and together they form the internal mosaic that is you. This unique composite represents what you love and what brings you joy, an ideal place to begin your journey toward manifesting what you desire.

Manifesting Moment to Moment

You have the power to change the lens with which you view your experience and your reality, and doing so will dramatically affect your potential for creating and manifesting those things that your soul desires. Whatever your personal belief about God, a higher power, or what we refer to in this book as the Universe, we urge you to embrace your spiritual truth in your manifestation process. In harmony with your spiritual beliefs, include the realization that you have a powerful influence over whatever happens in your life.

To guide you in your explorations and to assist in your success, we offer eight principles that will help you realize the extraordinary power you have to manifest. These principles work equally well in your personal life and in the corporate world, whether you are a business executive, an entrepreneur, or managing a household. Each chapter of this book explores in depth one of the following principles:

1. You Have a Unique Soul Mission. What is your essence? What lies at the very core of your being? How can your limitations serve you? By examining these questions, you can identify your gifts and what we call the "joy factor" that brings light to your soul. As your fears begin to fade, you start to manifest moment to moment that which you truly desire.

2. It's All About Energy. The power of your vibration affects every part of your life, and energy flows through you in multiple dimensions. Can you understand yourself as a complex unity of all these aspects, vibrating in harmony? When you develop the ability to work in harmony with all the forces available to you, you're able to materialize on the physical plane anything you wish.

3. Intuition Is the Magic Wand. How do you know what you know? If you use just your logical mind, then you are limiting your knowledge. Go beyond your linear understanding and discover seven elements to expand your intuitive self. The more you trust your intuition, the faster you can assess a situation and experience the natural flow of manifestation.

4. Your Belief and Your Story Do Not Define You and Can Be Changed. What is your story? How do you tell the narrative of your life, and what beliefs have grown out of your experience? These stories and beliefs are merely your mind's interpretation. They can also prevent you from being in the moment and taking action. As you change your story, you change your life.

5. Your Desire Forms the Basis of Every Manifestation. Is there an outcome you long for and yet somehow never experience? By examining your desire in every dimension, you can discover what may be blocking the manifestation of your dreams. If your desire is in alignment with your essence, you need not be concerned with the "how to"—your desire will be manifested.

6. Intention Overcomes Every Obstacle. Intention is an extremely powerful tool. Neither logic nor life's circumstances will stand in its way. No matter what your material resources or station in life, your intention—when clear and focused and sustained—will ensure the manifestation of your soul's mission.

7. You Have the Power to Clear, Heal, and Reinvent Constantly. When you carry unnecessary baggage in your life, such as clutter in your space or mental worries, your life force becomes drained. What are you holding on to that is preventing you from manifesting what you want? This clutter must be cleared for you to be able to focus on your intent and achieve what you desire. Clearing the energy of the chakras will enhance your vitality and magnify your ability to create the life you want.

8. Your Inner Guidance Knows the Path to Creating Life Balance. Where do you find the answer to the continuing challenges life presents? How do you choose among the array of opportunities that will grow as you begin to manifest your destiny moment to moment? Accessing your chakras and the five elements will help you find the answers within yourself.

We conclude by helping you fill a backpack with the tools you have discovered during your encounter with this book. They represent all of the new strengths you will need as you continue to manifest moment to moment. Make these skills a part of your daily life by participating fully in the Claim It! exercises provided for every principle.

Believe You Can

Throughout the book you will meet dozens of people who can provide inspiration for you as you go forward. In that vein, we would like to introduce you to Sophia. Her name means "wisdom," and as you will see, it suits her very well.

Sophia began studying the harp at age 9. She loved to perform and learned at an early age how to compose. On stage, she had a natural charisma and elegance that enthralled her audiences. When she was 11 years old, Sophia was diagnosed with muscular dystrophy. Many doctors told her that she wouldn't be able to continue to play harp, but Sophia chose to disagree with them and kept practicing.

At the age of 14, Sophia performed for millions of viewers on a nationally televised telethon. She played a piece she had composed, entitled "Believe You Can!" Her performance touched the hearts of thousands of children who had her same disease, and she empowered them to see that, with the right attitude, anything was possible.

When Sophia began studying harp, she didn't know where her journey might take her, but she knew she loved the harp and she practiced every day. By following her passion, she inspired millions of children and adults to go beyond their limitations. And she accomplished all of this by age 14!

Each of us is responsible for our own reality. The superhighway to manifesting the life you desire rests within you. It is not conditional upon anyone or anything else. Rather than choosing based on what others will think, or what effect your action will have, all you need to do is to follow your truth, your joy, as Sophia did. It's easy to say, "I can't." Sophia is the living proof of the statement: *If you believe, you can.*

Think of what happens when a rock is thrown into a pond. The ripples that result touch every part of the pond. Similarly, any small change that you incorporate in your life will have a wide impact as all the repercussions of that action are felt. When these changes are aligned with your soul mission, as you will explore in the following chapter, they will dramatically affect your power to manifest.

The place to begin is within. The time to begin is now.

You Have a
Unique Soul Mission

You have a specific purpose in life, and a part of you—right here, right now—knows exactly what that purpose is. You can communicate with that part, your soul, knowing that it can guide you in a way that will make your life the most meaningful, authentic, and joy-filled. This chapter will put you back in touch with your soul so that you can move toward manifesting at the highest level, moment to moment.

What Is the Soul?

The idea of the soul has roots deep in human history, and it is often associated with life source. The ancient Egyptians, for example, thought the soul included a vital spark that distinguished between the living and the dead. Thousands of years later, a Massachusetts physician named Duncan MacDougall weighed six bodies moments before and moments after death, finding a loss of 21 grams in each body, which he associated with the departure of the soul.

Although MacDougall published his findings in 1907 in the *Journal of American Medicine,* his quest for physical evidence of the soul's existence remains open. Nevertheless, most Western religions continue to hold that every person has a soul that joins the body before birth and departs from the body at death, moving on to enjoy an immortal life of some description.

Hindu philosophy sees it somewhat differently: The soul stands outside the stream of time so that it exists as one continuous entity before, during, and after the individual human life. Some believe that our soul decides to come to Earth and, according to some traditions, chooses its human family. The yogis have written that the soul enters into the womb of a mother in the 120th day of pregnancy.

At the heart of these varying beliefs about the soul is a central concept: *Every human being has a soul, and that includes you.* The soul is the core of your being, invincible and always intact. When you feel tired, overwhelmed, or discouraged, you may be failing to tap into the unlimited energy of your soul. The energy, vitality, and resources of your soul are endless and always available to you.

Of particular importance to manifesting moment to moment are three elements of the soul: your essence, your gifts, and your life lesson. By exploring how these elements contribute, you can uncover your soul mission and experience a life in which you are continuously manifesting moment to moment, radiating a joy that fills you and touches everyone who comes in contact with you.

Your Essence

Your essence is the blueprint of your being, defined by a very subtle blend of energy, as we will see in Principle 2. Everyone you meet is touched by your essence whether they are aware of it or not. How many times have you been attracted to someone in a group, even though you have never talked to them before? You sense/feel/know an urge to be in their presence—you are drawn to their essence, and you may feel it the moment they walk into a room.

Your essence is your foundation. Everything on the physical plane starts with a vibration—a thought, a desire, a dream. This is a concept we will discuss more fully in Principle 2. Your essence is the vibration that defines you.

In philosophy, *essence* is the inward nature or true substance of a being. Think about how we use the word in everyday conversation and you'll get an idea:

"The essence of our relationship is trust in each other."

"The smell of newly mown grass is the essence of summer in the suburbs."

"This oil is an essence—you will want to dilute it to use."

Now let's apply that thinking to people. The essence of Martin Luther King, Jr., was determination and courage. Mother Teresa's essence of compassion continues to impact our world long after her death. The Dalai Lama says his "religion is kindness," and perhaps kindness is also his essence. Essence is a quality you can't always put into words because words are tools of your brain and intellect. Essence can be experienced more directly—physically, emotionally, and spiritually.

When we hear truly magnificent artists onstage, we can feel that they are tapping into their essence. We may not remember what was played or sung, but we will remember the experience of seeing them share their essence. They are saying: "I am this, I believe this, it brings me joy." As a result, it brings us joy, too.

Sometimes we lose sight of our essence during the day-to-day routine of our lives, preoccupied with the hundreds of decisions, large and small, that we have to make. Very often, these decisions are made based on habits, obligations, and expectations that we put on ourselves, as well as social pressures or demands from bosses, children, loved ones. If our decisions and actions are not based on our personal truth, they will not reflect our essence. We will experience this as a sort of internal dissonance.

The more you act from your place of essence, the more powerful and fulfilled you will be. You will experience ease and flow and an empowering freedom with your decisions and actions. You will be in harmony with your inner core. Discovering this core strength offers important life insights and propels you toward manifesting that which will bring you true happiness.

Your essence is always perfect. It is without judgment and censure. It is eternal and transcends time and space. You may find it difficult to pick a word to define it, but you will know instinctively that this is your truth. You may need to look hard to find it. As we grow up, we tend to lose touch with our essence in the clutter of negative thoughts and worries, ideas about "how things are" that we pick up from schooling or our social circle's views of appropriateness. Our behavior begins to reflect what we "should do" rather than "who we are."

As children we often have ideas and dreams of what we want to accomplish in life. Sometimes these are expressed verbally, played out in games, or presented in artwork. While we are young, these early dreams can flourish apart from society's results-oriented demands and pressure to achieve. It is illuminating to remember back to ideas and images that we had as children. Isn't it true that often they are the purest thoughts and desires that we have ever had? The following exercise may help you recover the essence of the child you once were.

⋅≼ Claim It! The Eyes of a Child ≽⋅

1. Find a quiet space where you will be uninterrupted. Open your manifesting journal.

2. Write in each of the questions shown below, and then add answers. You don't have to follow any particular order. And don't struggle—above all, don't think of what your parents wanted or what they've told you about your childhood. Just stick to the questions.

- *When I was young, what did I want to be when I grew up?*

- *What did I find appealing about this?*

- *As I think back to my childhood, what was I doing or thinking when I was especially happy?*

- *Who made a strong impression upon me?* (This could have just been an acquaintance or somebody who passed through your life briefly.)

- *What was it about this person that I found so inspiring?*

3. Now look back at what you've written and take some deep breaths. Ask yourself:

- *What have I incorporated into my life that echoes those things I was attracted to as a child?*

- *What have I lost track of, and why?*

While some of the ideas that you were strongly attracted to as a child may lose their significance, others will continue to be part of your life—sometimes in a big way.

CARROL'S ESSENCE

One day, I was walking along the sidewalk on the way to a recording studio in Tucson, Arizona, to record a solo harp CD. Beside the sidewalk, I saw a baby bird that had fallen out of its nest. Although I was in a hurry, I knew that if I left the bird where it was, it would die. I found a shoebox and placed it inside, carrying it with me to the studio.

It almost drove the recording engineer crazy that the recording kept getting interrupted by shrill cries from the hungry baby bird. Each time the recording stopped, I fed the baby bird and, as it fell back asleep, continued to record the harp music. The recording went forward, but every time the baby bird called out that it was hungry, I stopped the music so I could feed it. Between the interruptions and the occasional cheeping of the bird, the sound engineer was exasperated.

The CD was a success. Many years later, however, what I value most from that day is the fact that I saved the bird's life. It can be hard to put your own essence into words. I think my essence is vitality and the belief that all things are possible. I'm always going toward life—that's my only direction. As much as I valued my harp performance, it was not as important as saving the bird. I got so much joy from doing that—and even years later, I can feel it.

Carrol's joy in saving the baby bird underscores the fact that her action was aligned with her essence. Joy is also an emotion that points in the direction of our soul's gifts.

Your Gifts

Our essence is expressed in our gifts, which you can think of as your essence in motion, interacting with others. When you share the qualities of who you are—your essence—you are giving the gift of who you are to the world around you.

We are born with gifts. A gift is what gives us joy. We often think of our talents as gifts, but the two aren't the same. A talent is what we are good at. It is what we have practiced and mastered. There may be some crossover, but the two are not identical. The fact that you do something well isn't what defines your gift. In fact, it may be your talent.

Carrol had an experience that may help you distinguish between *talent* and *gift*.

CARROL'S GIFT

I was born in Grande Prairie, Alberta, one of the north-ernmost communities in Canada. At age four, I decided I wanted to play the harp—in fact, I wanted to be one of the best harpists in the world.

Who knows why? As my grandmother remembers it, she often read me a story called *The Little Lost Angel*. Coming down from heaven on Christmas Eve, the angel starts giving away her possessions. A lame boy receives her wings so that he can move, and a crying woman gets her harp "to make her happy." According to Grandmother, every time she read the angel's words—"Here, I will give you my harp. It will make you happy"—I said, "Ahh! I want to play the harp."

My parents were more than encouraging. My father sent to Toronto for a harp and an instruction book—in French. No one in my hometown spoke French, but my father gave French-speaking guests at the hotel he owned a free room in return for translating a page for me. When I was nine, I started making a 16-hour round-trip bus ride by myself to Edmonton to take lessons, and by the time I was 14, I was the principal harpist with the Calgary Phil-harmonic. Today, I head one of the most respected harp departments in the world, at the University of Arizona, and I have made countless international concert tours with my harp.

Even at age four, I think I understood that the harp was my vehicle for expressing my gift: to uplift and bring joy to people with my harp.

For Carrol, her talent for playing the harp flowed directly from her essence, and it interacted naturally with her gift. This is not always true. Your gifts flow through you as gifts to others. Your talents, on the other hand, are often developed at an early age as ways to achieve practical ends. Because children need safety and recognition, they develop specific behaviors. For example, you may have decided very early (often due to positive reinforcement) to be the smart one, the caregiver, the organizer, or the pleaser. A wide range of behaviors can earn you the safety and recognition you need.

Very quickly you mastered skills that supported this talent, and then you started to attract situations that required those particular skills. This led to a comfort level in your competence, and in the short term, you may have enjoyed the success of these endeavors. However, as you developed further, despite social and financial recognition for these skills, you may have found the same activity lacking in satisfaction, energy, enthusiasm, and joy.

People may pursue a talent because it pleases someone else in their life or because it brings money, social recognition, or other rewards. This can be a hollow achievement if it doesn't touch your soul and rejuvenate you. Basing your life on your talent instead of your gift can lead to being "very successful and unhappy." Tejpal provides an example:

TEJPAL'S GIFT

I was an executive coach working with large companies internationally. Even though I was very successful, this scenario seemed to constrict my creativity, and I longed for a deeper connection to my soul mission. I took a leap of faith and went back to school to become an energy healer and yoga teacher. This dramatic shift allowed me to express my essence with tremendous joy.

Like Tejpal, when you share your gift, you experience a sense of joy, enthusiasm, and excitement. In fact, the more you give of your gift, the more you *want* to give. When you share your gift, there is a constant flow of abundance, and you receive as much or more than you give. You are empowered and energized, as opposed to depleted and empty.

Longing to Belong

Another issue that can stand between us and the expression of our gifts is the powerful human desire to belong, to be loved, to fit in and be accepted. This may prevent us from honoring our uniqueness and doing what brings us the most joy. We wonder what people will think and what reaction they will have to our choices.

When "what you think they think" becomes your reality, it can cause you to feel fear or anxiety. Energy and time are wasted wondering, *What do they think of me?* In fact, you can't really know what others think. This natural fear of being judged and rejected presents a conundrum. You want to be special and unique, but not at the price of not fitting in. It is also natural to want others to validate and agree with your choices.

The best way to fit in and be accepted, however, is to be joyful and radiate who you really are and what you believe. As long as you are happy with your own choices, you can be supported, loved, and welcomed by people who don't understand you, or even those who disagree with you.

Identifying Your Joy Factor

In the same way that we may lose touch with our essence, we may also lose sight of our gifts as we move into adulthood. Preoccupied with earning a living, pleasing others, and finding our place in society, we can become disconnected from the gifts that flow from our essence.

As you might guess from what we've been saying, joy is the treasure map that will guide you to the place your gifts may be buried. This exercise can help you begin the search.

⚡ Claim It! Where Is Your Joy? ⚡

List a series of activities that you perform regularly. Include elements from all parts of your life, work-related and otherwise. List them down the side of a page in your journal, and string the numbers 1 to 10 across the top.

Now evaluate your joy factor for each activity (10 being the most joyful). The following is the list and evaluation that Carrol made:

Activity Joy Factor:	1	2	3	4	5	6	7	8	9	10
Teach harp							x			
Participate in university committees	x									
Musical composition										x
Give workshops										x
Writing and publishing								x		
Play concerts									x	
Yoga							x			
Administration, secretarial	x									
Apply for grants	x									
International networking					x					
Spend time with family										x
Healing, Personal coaching									x	

Tejpal's chart looks like this:

Activity Joy Factor:	1	2	3	4	5	6	7	8	9	10
Working one-on-one with clients										x
Giving lectures										x
Writing and publishing								x		
Giving workshops										x
Teaching yoga										x
Bike riding									x	
Gardening								x		
Playing golf								x		
Cooking								x		
Networking		x								
Editing web pages	x									
Administrative/ secretarial	x									

Now create and fill in your own chart. If you find activities with a joy factor of 5 or less (such as Carrol's participation in university committees or Tejpal's work on editing web pages), we recommend you consider limiting your time spent on that activity.

Keep checking in with yourself. Are you operating from a place of joy? Do you trust yourself? Realize that if you are okay, everyone is okay. If your soul is at peace, those around you will mirror back to you that sense of serenity.

Trust Your Joy

Activities that bring you joy—that enhance what we call your "joy factor"—can help you see the parts of your life that are in harmony with your gifts and your essence. Everyone desires more joy in life. Your joy factor will be a keystone as we move forward to determining your soul mission and how you can manifest it in the world from moment to moment.

When you express your essence and your gifts, you access pure joy and radiance. Everyone around you will bask in the glow. Here are the stories of two people who chose to trust the joy and change their lives to enhance it.

When Cathy's husband, Joe, became housebound as the result of a serious and chronic illness, Cathy struggled to find inner peace and joy when she really felt trapped and resentful. When she decided to face her inner turmoil, she realized how much Joe's illness was at the center of everything in her life. So she decided to put her attention on something else. Saying yes to what brought her pleasure, Cathy revisited an early love of painting and later became a yoga teacher, which she has loved. She hired a caregiver to help with Joe. No longer burdened by her resentment and his own guilt, Joe also experienced new joy as he watched her life becoming more and more rewarding.

At the age of 37, George's life was running on an unfulfilling and lonely track. He spent the day at the office and returned home to watch television alone. To cope with his unhappiness, George developed a drinking problem. Eventually, his discomfort drove him to search for different answers. As he explored his soul calling, he realized that his true passion was for animals and nature. He looked into local organizations and volunteered at shelters for homeless animals. As he aided in rescuing animals, he felt a great sense of belonging and of joy, participating in something bigger than himself. Eventually, that led to a job in a new field that brings him pleasure—all because of his willingness to follow his passion and the calling of his soul. And his addictive behaviors are no longer a part of his life.

Your Life Lesson

The concept of a life lesson is apparent in many spiritual traditions ranging from Christianity to Buddhism, building a consensus that human beings are on Earth to grow, to learn, and to be uplifted. The human spirit is by nature unlimited, creative, and expansive. Onto this perfect template, life brings experiences that can cause us to create specific reactive behaviors that are out of harmony with the original structure. Each person faces at least one unique challenge in their lifetime. This challenge will show up over and over until we learn the true lesson that is embedded within it: our life lesson. For some the life lesson may be related to money. For others it may lie with health, relationships, self-acceptance, or a vast array of other issues. Our life lesson is the newfound understanding we gain when we recognize and become accountable for our reactive behaviors and move toward change. It can often be identified by looking at the behaviors that limit us.

Our Limiting Behaviors

Most of us have a number of behaviors that seem almost automatic, where we respond to events or experiences in limiting or negative ways—and we just can't seem to help ourselves.

Responding with anger, saying yes when we mean no, seeing ourselves as the victim in our relationships, lacking self-confidence, judging ourselves and others—all of these are reactive behaviors. Here are some examples:

Susan wants to help everybody, so she always commits herself to projects, even when she knows she really doesn't have the time for them. This always leaves her feeling depleted, but then before you turn around, she's doing it again. She feels unable to alter the sequence of events. *Why?* she asks herself.

John likes to present a strong, positive image. Rather than let others see that he might be vulnerable, he struggles through anxiety and fear, unable to ask for help. He always says that he is fine, and at the same time, he feels a deep sense of isolation. Even though he recognizes the pattern, he can't seem to undo it. He feels that his life is careening out of control.

Helen constantly hears an internal dialogue that says she is not good enough. She second-guesses herself at every turn, then gets angry that she can't make decisions quickly. What if she does the wrong thing? She feels powerless and paralyzed.

You may feel a kinship with one of these people, or you may have a different issue. You may, in fact, relate a little to all three. Whatever your personal issues may be, chances are, one reactive behavior is the dominant note in your personal song.

An *anomaly* is defined as a deviation from the common rule, an irregularity. Personal anomalies may take on many forms. These range from eating disorders to addictions, from self-sacrifice to being judgmental or resentful. One behavior is usually more upsetting to you than the others. This is the behavior that is the key to your life lesson. You feel so much discomfort because the behavior is out of tune with your essence. In fact, the more discomfort you feel, the surer you can be that it represents a life lesson that, when explored, will have far-reaching impact upon you and your voyage of self-discovery. If you can identify and overcome it, you can bring more harmony into your life and a potential for a richer and truer manifestation.

Ask yourself: *Which of my behaviors would I most like to eliminate?* The following exercise can also help you see what limiting anomalies are holding you back from experiencing your highest potential.

⁙ Claim It! Then Disclaim It ⁙

1. List several behaviors in your manifestation journal you've watched yourself do over and over that limit your potential.

2. Examine your list. Which one of these behaviors makes you feel the worst? Which one do you dislike the most?

3. Assess your relationship with this behavior. When you think of it, do you . . .

- Go into blaming yourself

- Feel worthless

- Feel powerless

- Shut down

- Deny

- Become defensive

- Hear your internal dialogue beating yourself up

- Go into compulsive behavior, such as drinking or overeating

- Other experiences: _____

4. Now, having already altered your experience by exploring it rather than just reacting, take an even closer look:

- What are the facts of your experience? Putting aside your feelings and reactions, what actually happened, step-by-step?

- How could you change your approach when you find yourself in a similar situation again?

- If you could overcome this thought or behavior pattern, how would your life change? How would you feel about yourself?

Once you have identified your limiting behavior, you have a choice. You can continue to respond in restrictive and reactive ways, allowing this behavior to remain a habit that prevents you from experiencing what you want from life. You can try to ignore the problem or blame it on other people, and stay numb. Or you can accept the life lesson that is part of this debilitating obstacle and view it as an opportunity to speed up your learning and move to a more powerful level of manifestation.

The circumstances that first created the limiting behaviors that are part of your life lesson lie in the past. What matters is the present: how these behaviors affect you today by restricting your energy, creativity, and life possibilities. Your energy becomes obstructed, light cannot enter your soul, and your view of the world becomes cloudy. But you don't have to remain in this cycle.

We're talking about manifesting *moment to moment.* While it's true that this may be *the way you've always done things* or *the way you see the world,* every moment brings with it the potential to change your direction. What you've done in the past doesn't matter. What you do now is all that counts. Following is a technique that can help you to overcome the magnetic pull of old thought and behavior patterns and release the memories and beliefs that no longer serve you.

⋇ Claim It! Release and Renew ⋇

1. To begin, find a quiet place where you can be undisturbed, and take a few moments to calm yourself and focus on the moment.

2. Recall something that overwhelms or stresses you. Perhaps you had an uncomfortable conversation with a member of the family, or something that happened at work still bothers you and drains your energy when you think of it. Concentrate on this thought as you inhale and hold your breath.

3. With the third finger of your right hand, tap the following points. Tap each point lightly five or six times as you access your troublesome memory:

- Eyebrow, at the beginning of the brow near the nose

- Side of the eye, the bone at the outer edge of the eye

- Under the eye, on the bone that forms the lower eye socket

- Just under the nose

- Between your lower lip and chin

4. Exhale the breath fully while you tap your collarbone with thumb and third finger. As you do this, say, "I release this with gratitude."

5. Recall the problem again, inhale, and repeat the full sequence several times until your discomfort is diminished.

This technique uses the meridian system to release the memory and replace it with gratitude, which is incompatible with tension and stress. The inspiration for this exercise came from Emotional Freedom Techniques (EFT), an alternative medical practice developed by Gary Craig in the 1990s. Tapping designated points on the body in a prescribed order releases emotions and energy. Emotions have been called energy in motion, and they can become trapped as energy in the body. Releasing that energy can help you overcome stress and let go of the memory of the event that put it there.

The Hidden Blessing

In each challenge we face, we can find a golden truth, a precious insight. Every obstacle offers a great opportunity for growth. Our biggest challenge is our best teacher and offers our life lesson. As you conquer this challenge, you gain the experience you need to become the best possible teacher on how to overcome the challenge or to let it go. Your teaching will have a tremendous influence because it is born out of your experience and your truth. Everyone has a teacher within, and you teach the best what you most need to learn.

Philip is a chief executive officer who sought help. For 50 years, he had been extremely successful in his business life. From the outside, he seemed like the most calm, consistent person you can imagine. He achieved this greatness, however, by ignoring his own needs, again and again, in every situation. Inside he was miserable, and as his career came to a close, he wanted to do something that gave him pleasure. His life lesson was to listen to his own needs; he had to learn to trust the internal voice that was struggling to get his attention. As he discovered that truth and began to live accordingly, he turned his wisdom outward: Now he helps business executives create a life balance that includes self-reward and pleasure.

The sharing of your personal wisdom is extremely rewarding and is an important part of your soul mission. Besides putting our behavior in greater harmony with our essence, identifying our life lesson brings with it a blessing that may not be obvious at first. It points us in the direction of our soul mission, the work we were born to do. Our soul mission, universally, involves service—not only to others, but also to ourselves.

We Are on Earth to Serve

Nobel Peace Prize winner Albert Schweitzer once wrote: "The purpose of human life is to serve and to show compassion and the will to help others." As you search for your own truth, include in your vision that we are all on Earth to serve others—in a way that serves us. Service is imbedded in the DNA of human cells, that unique chemical configuration that is the scientific essence of your identity. No two people have the same DNA, and no two people have the same service mission.

Service, or helping others, is a natural part of human nature, according to Michael Tomasello, co-director of the Max Planck Institute for Evolutionary Anthropology, in Leipzig, Germany. In his book *Why We Cooperate,* Tomasello states that "when infants 18 months old see an unrelated adult whose hands are full and who needs assistance opening a door or picking up a dropped clothespin, they will immediately help." This internal desire to assist others forms a part of our human soul mission.

The notion of service is often misunderstood to mean only giving, not receiving. But actually, service involves both giving and receiving. When you serve in a way that serves you, that gives you pleasure and uplifts you, it is the ultimate win-win situation. For many people this idea can be challenging because of a belief that when you honor your own needs, you are selfish. But, in fact, it is only as you discover a way to serve that fulfills and supports you personally that you will realize the full power within you.

Your Soul Mission

As you discover your way to serve, your essence, your gifts, and your life lesson, you are awakening your awareness to your soul mission. This soul mission will be consistent throughout your lifetime, although the form it takes may vary. For example, if your soul mission involves justice, you may be a lawyer for the first ten years of your life and then shift to being a teacher or a writer, exploring the same concept from a different vantage point.

When you allow yourself to use your life lesson, gifts, and essence to manifest your soul mission and serve in the world, you will find that your peace and joy grow exponentially. Your limiting behaviors may not disappear, but they will fade into the background, and you will have more energy and gratitude toward life. The benefits of manifesting your soul mission are endless. Often, this mission will grow out of your life lesson. Philip is one example, and following are some others:

> Until she turned the corner toward recognizing her essence and her gifts, Gina was always expecting the worst. That was her life lesson. She was frequently discouraged, and she could be hurt and disappointed easily. Her soul mission is to help people learn to not take things too seriously.

Odette has always struggled with self-worth. Although she won many awards, she never felt worthy. Recognizing her life lesson, she has set out on a soul mission of teaching others how to believe in themselves and their abilities.

For much of his life, Charles had stuttered, a physical disability that grew out of his life lesson: that he wasn't worthy of being heard. He worked hard to overcome his disability and now is a nationally respected announcer. As he leads his radio show, he spotlights stories of people and issues that need to be heard and known. His work has touched and inspired many people.

Charles is a great example of the courage it can take to engage your essence and gifts in the pursuit of your soul mission. He was beset by a reasonable fear, based on his previous experience, that he would not be able to express himself clearly, and yet he moved forward.

Honoring Your Fears

When you see yourself obsessing over answers to every question you have regarding your soul mission, slow down for a moment, close your eyes, take a deep breath, and notice how you feel. You are most likely experiencing fear. Fear does not need to limit you in manifesting your soul journey. It is not inherently bad. The most important thing is to accept your fears, not be afraid of them. Avoiding fear is an illusion and restricts you in your journey. When you are afraid of your fears, they take over and drive your life. When you accept your fears, you stay connected to your essence and are therefore open to manifesting in alignment with your soul mission.

If you want to do something and you don't do it well—the first or second time, or ever—that doesn't mean that you are incompetent in that arena. All it means is that this particular experience did not work. Think of Edison and his many unsuccessful attempts at making a lightbulb. In fact, the world only remembers his success.

In athletics, the ultimate winners are those who keep trying—and failing—until they perfect their physical efforts and knowledge of the sport. To be a winner, you have to try many, many times. Those who become winners were not afraid to follow their dreams. Successful athletes face their fears, learn from each experience, and always keep going toward their goal. The same is true of many respected leaders in business and politics, who experience failure on a regular basis. What makes them successful is their ability to respond, adapt, reinvent, and move on.

Many successful people start with an inspiration, a goal that they're moving toward, like the four-year-old Carrol who wanted to be a famous harpist. That four-year-old didn't know every step along the path she would take before she set out on the journey. Nevertheless, she felt a tremendous enthusiasm for her desire and that helped her muster the energy to reach her destination. Your joy factor can serve the same role as a compass, pointing you in the direction of your soul mission wherever you happen to find yourself in life. Sometimes the literal left brain needs the artistic interpretation of the right brain in order to help you find where your soul's north may be located.

Getting a Picture in Mind

Art offers a unique opportunity for self-expression that reaches beyond logic and reason. Often, if you have a perplexing problem that you are not able to solve, taking a break to do some art will allow the right side of your brain to formulate answers that would otherwise be unavailable to you when accessing the linear left brain. Try this out as you consider your soul mission and move toward the manifestation of your desire:

⊰ Claim It! Soul Collage ⊱

1. Find pictures that appeal to you and seem to express your essence. You can do this over a period of time, as you read magazines and newspapers, or you can put the reading material aside and search for images in one session.

2. Collect your tools: a large piece of heavy paper or poster board, scissors, and glue.

3. Assemble the images in a way that pleases you. Don't do a lot of thinking. Move the images around and stop when it looks or feels right; then glue it down.

4. You may use crayons or felt-tip pens to draw on the images or to write words or messages to yourself.

5. Celebrate the personal expression you have made and keep it in a place where you will see it often. Feel free to add images as your soul mission becomes clearer and clearer.

As you get a clearer picture of your soul's destination, you may find that your fears begin to fade on their own, replaced by an enthusiasm for your gifts and an energy that comes when you are acting in tune with your essence. This is how manifestation works. Keep in mind that it's happening moment to moment. All you need is readiness to move forward.

In the next chapter, we will invite you to a new understanding of how your being fits into the Universe of energy and help you to let the flow of this energy manifest itself in your life moment to moment.

It's All About Energy

Everything that exists in this world, whether in its solid form or thought form, consists of energy. The building we live in, the floor under our feet—and the sturdy legs that take us down seemingly solid sidewalks—are all energy in motion. At a molecular level, quantum physics tells us, everything is composed of atoms; and in those atoms, protons, electrons, and neutrons are engaged in an electromagnetic and chemical dance that is the source and reflection of all the energy in the Universe.

You, too, are vibrating with energy. Not only your physical body, but also the thoughts you are having as you read this, the surprise or doubt you feel in response, the spiritual recognition you may sense—all of those are vibrating with energy as well. When you're sad, your energy field is different than when you're happy.

You are alive with energy at several different levels. When your different dimensions of energy—physical, emotional, mental, heart, and spiritual—are vibrating at different speeds and in different patterns, you may feel out of sorts. When they are aligned, you experience a sense of harmony; the energy flows freely through you, enabling the highest levels of manifestation, moment to moment.

Like quantum physicists, healers also understand that energy underlies all existence. Disease starts as energy, then creates distortions that move symptoms into the physical level. Using this knowledge, healers can help people return to harmony in their energy field. In fact, healers can access your energy field even if you live 3,000 miles away. As they work, energy healer and patient will feel a shift as the energy flow or vibration comes into harmony. It's palpable.

TEJPAL'S STORY

It is 7:30 P.M. in Tucson, and my client, Jen, is in Perth, Australia, where it's 10:30 A.M. the next day. Jen has had a headache for the past two weeks, and I am giving a distance healing over the phone. My first assessment reveals an energetic obstruction in her neck, and her spine is tilted to the left starting at Lumbar 2. I can experience Jen as if we were in the same room together.

As I clear her energy field and energetically realign her spine, Jen feels a tremendous relief. We talk about the emotional components related to her physical stress, particularly her business partnership. As Jen realizes the source of her discomfort, she is able to envision what changes must be made in her business. Her headache is gone, and she is excited to implement her new ideas.

Although you may not become an energy healer, you can learn how to read energy and to understand how it is working for you—or not—in your life. In Principle 1, we learned that you will feel harmony only when you align your life with your soul's essence, when you express your soul's gifts, and when you learn your life lesson and translate it into your soul mission. In this chapter, we discuss some tools you can use to accomplish these goals. Making use of these suggestions, you'll become much more powerful in your day-to-day life, manifesting what you truly want moment to moment.

How Energy Affects Your Life

You get a speeding ticket. You're drawn into an unnecessary argument with your spouse or children. No matter which piece of your life you're attending to at a given time, you feel distracted. It's hard to concentrate. What's happening is that you are out of vibrational alignment. The sensation of being out of harmony with yourself, with your own soul, can feel like descending into a black hole. The answer, the antidote, lies in oneness: unity of mind, body, and spirit. This is the purpose of yoga and other mind/body practices. In fact, *yoga* is translated as *yoke,* meaning union. Everything becomes just one.

This unity also comes into play in your relationships with the world around you. Every aspect of your life is affected by vibration—the kind of music you like, the friends you attract, the place you live, and the clothes you feel good wearing. The importance of your energy field and its impact on your ability to manifest moment to moment cannot be overstated.

By enhancing your awareness of your energy, you will find that you have more options as you manifest moment to moment. You will become more sensitive to your environment, and you will be able to make more conscious choices. You will also begin to sense when you are "stuck": when energy is no longer moving easily or you are out of vibrational alignment.

Human beings are creatures of habit. There's a natural tendency for us to access and process information in the same way we always have. This traditional way of thinking can be limiting and can cause us to become "stuck." It's similar to what happens when the needle of an old-fashioned turntable runs into dirt or a scratch in an LP record. The turntable is still spinning, but because the grooves are blocked, the music repeats again and again, unable to move forward.

Getting stuck is often accompanied by *internal dialogue*, which sends messages of "I can't," "I'm not good enough," and so on. The more often you experience this sequence, the more of a habit it becomes. You need a way to break the unproductive patterns that have become your habits. In this chapter, we'll describe a variety of tools you can use to bring your energy patterns into alignment and create more flow.

Using Breath to Move Forward

Breath is the fastest way to change your energy patterns. If you change your breath, everything changes: your experience and your relationship to things. Because of this, you will find many exercises throughout this book that focus on breathing and show how you can use it to move toward a clearer manifestation.

As you do these breath exercises on a regular basis, you will become more aligned and centered. A commitment of 40 days is often the key to transformation. This time interval is common to evoke change in different spiritual traditions. Lent, for example, is 40 days long, and in early Christianity, those who sought baptism had to cleanse themselves for 40 days.

Breath has the power to alter your behavior and your reactions, perhaps more than any other single element of your life because your breath is a reflection of who you are. When you breathe, you take in *Prana,* a Yogic word that means "life force," not only oxygen but also an ultimate vibration that is essential to living. Deep breathing helps you to remain calm and prevents you from overreacting, whereas shallow breathing promotes a disconnection from your body that may lead to anxiety and depression. When your mind is in charge, your choices are very limited.

How do you inhale? Inhaling reflects your ability to receive and to engage. Exhaling is a great metaphor in life, relating to expressing your truth and releasing. When you exhale, you clear and create space so that you can revitalize yourself and be open to receive what the Universe has to offer you. The following exercise offers a powerful tool to assist you in establishing a vibrational harmony, which is a precursor to manifestation.

❊ Claim It! Just Breathe ❊

Part I

1. Sit comfortably in a place where you won't be disturbed.

2. Put your hand in the middle of your chest. Notice your breathing. How fast or slow do you breathe? Is your breath shallow or deep?

3. Pay attention to the transition between inhaling and exhaling. Relax your abdomen so your breath can move deeply into your body, allowing you to experience more energy and alignment.

4. Now release your hand, but remain aware of your breathing and the power it carries.

Part II

1. Breathe in and hold your breath.

2. Hold your breath in for a count of 5 to 10 seconds, extending that length as you become more comfortable. Eventually you may be able to hold it for 20 seconds.

3. Now exhale completely, and hold your breath out for the same count.

4. Suspending the breath after inhaling stimulates and intensifies your energy level. Suspending the breath after you exhale allows you to experience a deep stillness and calm.

5. Continue this breathing pattern for three minutes.

Find time as often as possible during the day to repeat this exercise, especially if you're feeling pressured or upset. We urge you to mark off 40 days on your calendar and make this breathing exercise a daily habit for that period.

Where Do You Live?

The concept of "multiple bodies" has appeared for centuries in numerous spiritual and healing traditions ranging from Buddhism to Christianity. In Western culture, we relate to the three bodies or dimensions of mind, body, and spirit. Many aspects of these varying disciplines share a common understanding that we are much more than just a physical body and that each body interacts and affects each other.

We propose that there are five bodies through which you filter your life experiences: the physical body, emotional body, mental body, heart body, and spiritual body. Viewing your actions, thoughts, and feelings from the context of these bodies allows you to alter your perspective and open up to a diversity of otherwise unseen possibilities and opportunities.

These bodies or dimensions are interdependent, but looking at each dimension separately can help us understand how we can enhance our power to manifest the life we want. Viewing the five dimensions can help us see where our energy may be blocked or where energy patterns are misaligned. This, in turn, impacts our potential to manifest.

The Five Dimensions

Physical	The anatomy and physiology of the body as well as your physical sensations (relaxed, constricted, tense, spacious, etc.).
Emotional	The emotions you are experiencing: joy, sadness, anger, excitement, depression, fear, resentment, happiness, etc.

Mental	Your thoughts and the way you process information. Are you clear or confused? Steady or spinning?
Heart	The quality of your heart. The Institute of HeartMath has discovered that the energy field of the heart is 500 to 5,000 times bigger than the energy field of the brain. In different healing and spiritual traditions, the heart represents the bridge between physical and spiritual realities. Are you trusting, accepting, receiving, giving, compassionate, forgiving? Are you resentful, shut down, self-centered, etc.?
Spiritual	Your soul's essence. Is your life meaningful? Are you living your soul mission?

Understanding yourself as a composite of these five dimensions is a pathway to expansion and a tool that opens up the possibilities of manifestation. Each dimension is a different expression of your being, so that as you experience every situation, you will be able to comprehend and process in a deeper way. This allows you to be open and receptive to new opportunities.

Another benefit of being connected to all five of your bodies is that you can get new insights into seemingly insurmountable problems. Often a difficulty is just a result of becoming stuck in one thought pattern or imagined reality. Remember that you simultaneously hold many dimensions that are all interrelated. Your five bodies constantly interact with each other, as Tejpal has discovered.

TEJPAL'S STORY

For a couple of years, I was involved in road-bike racing. My very specific training program included workouts focusing on a particular cadence, power output, and heart rate. Part of this program was a recovery ride, an interval during which the biker backs off speed and power output, while the cadence remains high. During these intervals, I decided to monitor my heart rate and compare it to the thoughts and emotions I was experiencing. When I was visualizing myself winning the next race—and without pedaling harder—my heart rate would go up to 30 beats more per minute. My mental and emotional body affected my physical body.

You can take advantage of your multiple dimensions to become more sensitive and more creative, allowing your life force to manifest moment to moment. The following exercise will help you experience and develop the full spectrum of your potential. Revisit this exercise numerous times, and each time you do so, you will discover another layer of "you." Relax into this experience and empower yourself as you recognize your inherent power.

⊰ Claim It! Your Five Dimensions or Bodies ⊱

1. Sit in a quiet place, and keep in mind that your answers are within; allow yourself to access that knowledge.

2. Think about a particular situation in your life. It might be a stressful period of time in the recent past, an event that concerned you, or a decision that lies ahead of you.

3. Connect to your **physical body** as you consider this situation. What is your physical experience? Do you feel hot or cold? Do you feel tense or relaxed? Are there parts of your body that you are more aware of than others? Do you feel pressure, and if so, where? Can you feel your heartbeat? What about your breathing? Do you feel energized or lethargic?

4. After exploring your physical body, take a deep breath to clear your mind and be open to the next experience.

5. Now think about the same situation as you connect to your **emotional body.** What emotions do you experience? Do you have mixed or conflicting feelings? Are they strong or weak? Do you feel expansive and open, full of joy and expectation? Or do you feel constricted, tight, and fearful? Are you surprised by anything that comes up?

6. Take another deep breath and let go of the previous thoughts.

7. This time, concentrate on your **mental body** by noticing your thinking. Do you hear internal dialogue? Is there clarity or complexity? Do you experience confusion? Notice that each thought carries with it an emotion and a physical experience. Some of your thoughts will uplift you and support you to take action, while other thoughts can be debilitating and overwhelming.

8. Take another deep breath.

9. Become aware of your **heart body.** As you think of your situation, is your heart open or constricted? Do you feel pressure in any part of your heart center? How much can you let go of? If you are in pain or experiencing fear, your heart will contract and tense up. If you are experiencing joy and trust, your heart will open, and you will be better able to embrace and accept all opportunities for growth. What are you feeling: gratitude, forgiveness, openness, or acceptance? Simply observe without judgment.

10. Take another deep breath.

11. Connect to your **spiritual body.** This is your higher self, your soul's essence. Realize that this part of you is always present but not always recognized. The spiritual body can be viewed as your inner guidance, the teacher within. Much can be learned by accessing this part of you. Right now, do you feel an internal sense of warning or enthusiasm? Be open to receive wisdom that can help you.

12. Take a deep breath. Express gratitude for the information you've received.

What insights did you gain from this exercise? Which of the five dimensions or bodies was easiest for you to access? Did you notice any similarities or patterns between the different bodies? Often, you will find an association, such as between the physical and emotional bodies. You might think of a challenging emotional situation and experience a physical pain in a specific part of your body.

There is no right or wrong outcome from this exercise. No expectation that you need to meet. The exercise will probably be different every time you do it. Here's how one of our clients used the exercise to help her understand a problem:

Jill has been struggling with her boyfriend, Tim, and has spent endless hours complaining about their relationship without taking clear action. She feels he doesn't respect her, and sometimes he makes fun of her feelings. She also doesn't approve of his drinking habits. When she did the Five Dimensions exercise, this is what she discovered:

• *Physical:* She experienced lots of tension and heaviness in her back. She felt exhausted. She is surprised by the intensity of the experience in her physical body.

- *Emotional:* She experienced lots of frustration, deep sadness, and then fear.

- *Mental:* The experience of her physical body helped her understand that she needs to set clearer boundaries despite the fears. She realized that her fear of losing Tim has created lots of mental confusion.

- *Heart:* She is hopeful that this relationship can change for the better.

- *Spiritual:* She knows that the changes she is making to find more meaning and happiness in her life are where she needs to place her focus.

By doing this exercise, Jill understood that her fear of losing Tim was taking over her thinking and her actions. Through the information provided by the five different dimensions, she was able to look at the problem without being overwhelmed with it. She now was able to share her fears with Tim and work with him to create a better relationship.

Considering the five dimensions of your being is one way to access and fine-tune your energy field. Other methods help you achieve the same goal.

Explore Your Senses

Another way to experience flow in your life and to stop being stuck is by viewing your experience with a different part of the brain. The science of Neuro-Linguistic Programming (NLP) examines the ways your brain stores and retrieves information. *Neuro* refers to the nervous system, *linguistic* refers to the language that is used to communicate to the nervous system, and *programming* refers to the ability to create behavioral patterns that will achieve the outcomes we desire. This gets you unstuck!

Learning how your brain processes information and being able to alter your thought patterns also helps you to go beyond your limitations and thus to facilitate manifestation. It is a highly effective method for changing energy patterns that aren't serving you.

According to NLP, the three primary pathways or modes for processing our experiences are *Visual* (to see), *Auditory* (to hear), and *Kinesthetic* (to feel). As a human being, you have the potential to use all three of these modes, but often you will develop a leading mode or habitual way of thinking that you rely on most often. Learning how you habitually store and retrieve information is extremely valuable as you increase your potential to manifest.

The words you use are often a clue to which of the three modes you are accessing. A Visually oriented person will use phrases such as, "I *see* your point" or "*looks* like a good idea." Their ability to recall information will be enhanced if they see the information written down or have a picture in their mind's eye of something they want to remember. An Auditory person will remember hearing information and will use words such as, "*sounds* good to me" or "that *rings* true." A Kinesthetic person might say, "This *ties me up* in knots" or "that *feels* right to me." Kinesthetic involves both the sense of touch (feel the table) and emotions (I feel nervous).

Take a moment and think about how you process and recall information. If you leave your car in a parking garage, how do you remember where to find it? Do you visually remember the area in which you parked? Or do you say to yourself, *Row 5, last car,* which is auditory remembering? Or do you remember how it felt where you parked, kinesthetically sensing it was in one general direction, and far away or close to the entrance? Remembering you parked next to a big truck, by the way, is not a successful strategy because the truck might move and you will have no idea where to find your car!

Listen carefully to the way people around you speak. Notice what words they use and also what words you habitually use: Are they Kinesthetic, Visual, or Auditory in nature? As you realize what mode you use most often, it will clarify the way your mind processes and literally how you think. After you identify what your most comfortable mode is, try utilizing other modes. When you change the way you process, you get a new perspective on problems or difficulties. In addition, you can work on using other modes to store and retrieve information, which strongly affects your potential to remember information.

The Eyes Have It

One of the forefathers of Neuro-Linguistic Programming was Dr. Milton Erickson, a psychiatrist in Phoenix, Arizona, in the 20th century. He became famous because of his phenomenal success in treating phobic patients in a very short amount of time. For example, a claustrophobic person might walk many flights of stairs up to an appointment with Erickson, too fearful to ride in the elevator. At the end of one session, that same patient would get in the elevator with no anxiety, fears completely gone.

To discover what made Erickson so successful, two therapists from California, Richard Bandler and John Grinder, set up video cameras focused on Erickson and his patients. After close observation of the tapes, Bandler and Grinder concluded that the secret to Erickson's success was his awareness that the mind stores and processes information, both factual and emotional, in different sensory categories or submodalities. They determined that the positioning of the eyes as you recall the information indicates which modality is being accessed—in effect, how you are thinking.

A Visual person will look up; an Auditory person will look to the side, parallel with the ears; and a Kinesthetic person will look down and to the right. If the person is looking down and to the left, they are accessing "internal dialogue," or talking to themselves.

You'll need a partner for this next exercise, a conversation that will help both of you determine your primary way of processing material.

⟨ Claim It! See My Point? ⟩

1. Sit comfortably across from your partner, directing them to watch your eye movements as they ask you questions. They might begin with simple questions: "What is on the top shelf of your refrigerator?" or "How many windows are there in your home?" or "What is your favorite animal?" or "What does an ambulance sound like in London, England?"

2. As your partner listens, ask him or her to watch where your eyes move. Forget that anyone is watching your eye movements so you will get the most natural movements possible.

3. Now have your friend ask questions such as, "What do you want to manifest in ten years?" Your eye motions will suggest where you store your desire. Do you visualize what you want (such as a large house, a relationship, and so on) by looking up, or do you feel it as you move your eyes down and to the left?

4. As the conversation goes on, talk to your partner about something that concerns you, such as a troubling event, a problem you face, or a life direction you are considering; for example, what would you like to manifest in ten years?

5. Again, ask your partner to observe and record your eye movements. Sometimes this movement is subtle, so he or she will need to watch carefully.

6. Change roles and repeat the sequence.

Normally there will be one mode (either Visual, Auditory, or Kinesthetic) that you will access more often than any other mode, or at least, it will be the first mode that you go to when you are retrieving information.

If, for example, you're asked what is on the top shelf of your refrigerator, you would probably immediately look up and, in your mind's eye, see the fridge and everything that is sitting on the shelf. If you look up to access most of your answers, it means that you are "visually led" and primarily store your knowledge in the Visual mode. Sometimes your eyes will make a secondary move to another position. For example, after looking up and "seeing" your empty fridge, you might look down and to the left as you hear your internal dialogue say, *Oh yeah, I need to buy milk.*

Pay special attention to the mode you use when you talk about serious subjects—a problem or your desires for the future. Then deliberately examine the same issue using a different mode. Instead of visualizing what you want, for example, think about how it would sound or feel. By diversifying the way you access your desires, you open up new possibilities for manifesting them moment to moment.

Your Strong Suit

Since you are capable of processing in all three modes, using only your "leading mode" is extremely limiting. If something obstructs the information coming from that part of the brain, you would not be able to retrieve the information you need. In order to facilitate manifestation, learn to utilize all of your modes. To strengthen Visual, practice looking up and recalling images from your memory. To strengthen Auditory, recall exactly what a person says or recite poetry or memorize phone numbers by saying them out loud. To strengthen Kinesthetic, associate a feeling with anything you want to remember. Recall the sensation of petting a favorite animal, or the emotion when you did something extremely well and felt wonderful about yourself. Just like building strength in any muscle of the body, the more you use all the modes, the stronger each one will become.

As you learn to depend on all three modes, Visual, Auditory, and Kinesthetic, you have three times the potential to manifest moment to moment.

Triple-Channel Living

Winston Churchill was famous for remembering names. The reason he was so successful at this was because when he met someone he would repeat the person's name aloud (Auditory); visualize a picture of the person, perhaps remembering their red dress or blond hair (Visual); and with his finger, he would write the person's name on his thigh (Kinesthetic). In other words, he triple-channeled his learning process by using all three modes of Visual, Auditory, and Kinesthetic. This same technique is available to you.

Using only Kinesthetic to remember information can be problematic, especially in times of stress. Kinesthetic involves the emotions (how you feel), and so often a sensation of being overwhelmed will accompany a thought. Perhaps you cannot bring yourself to return phone calls. When you think of the call you need to make you immediately feel swamped, guilty, and unable to move (processing in Kinesthetic). Change how you are processing by switching to Visual mode. Look up as you think of the phone call you need to make. You will be able to see the telephone and envision yourself making the call. Immediately, you become unstuck.

This is a powerful tool for creating change. When you're stuck, the energy flow in your body is diminished. By altering your mode of perception, you can remove the blockage and free the energy you need to manifest moment to moment.

Claim It! Experiencing Through Kinesthetic, Visual, and Auditory

1. Find a quiet place where you'll be undisturbed.

2. Think of a challenging situation that is coming up for you.

3. As you look down and to the right to access through Kinesthetic, imagine yourself in the situation. How do you feel when you think of this? Where in your body do you feel the discomfort?

4. Now experience the same situation, but from a Visual perspective (looking up). See all the elements. Envision possible alternative actions such as someone helping you. Notice how much more of a flow of energy you have, and how solutions that were previously blocked by your Kinesthetic fear now become possible.

5. To experience your Auditory mode, look parallel with the horizon and toward your left ear. Remember words of advice from family and friends that might help you in this situation.

6. Still considering the challenge you face, focus on your internal dialogue. Are you saying to yourself, *I can't do that, I'm not good enough, I don't have enough time* (or money, expertise, and so forth)? If so, challenge that statement! Tell yourself: *What would I do if I knew the answer? Maybe I am good enough. Pretend I know what to do.*

There are two important elements to the strategy outlined in this exercise. First, recognize how you are thinking. Second, understand that you have the power and knowledge to change it. Visualizing a solution offers a stress-free answer and allows your energy to flow so that you can manifest moment to moment.

Here's another example. Suppose you are writing a report, and you discover that your internal dialogue (looking down and to the left) is sending negative messages: "I don't know how to begin." "I can't do this." Remember that you have three options:

- *Visual (eyes looking up or, for some people, staring straight ahead):* See yourself typing the last sentence of the report and then the whole project completed.

- *Auditory (eyes to the side at ear level):* Hear yourself discussing this project with a friend and telling him or her about it.

- *Kinesthetic (eyes down and to the right):* Put your fingers on the keyboard and start to type—whatever you feel like typing. The touch of the keys alone may unblock your energy. Feel how wonderful it is to have achieved your goal.

Your success in manifesting moment to moment depends on the free flow of energy, and there are many ways to achieve this. One key is to harness your internal dialogue and halt self-judgment.

Judging Versus Witnessing

No matter how you are processing, self-judgment is self-defeating. In Kinesthetic terms, you feel inadequate. In Visual terms, you see yourself as incapable. In Auditory terms, you hear, "That was stupid!" In each case, judgment prevents you from altering your paradigm and viewing the situation from another mode. It also blocks your energy and leaves you unable to move forward.

When you judge, you shut down. Your soul's essence is smothered by your thoughts and your self-condemnation. Judgment causes you to freeze, preventing the flow of information and insights necessary for you to learn from any experience. Judgment is reactive. It doesn't allow for creative problem solving. It blocks the energy essential to manifesting moment to moment.

Judgment cements you into a rigid, unbending stance from which it is very difficult to move and to manifest. The second you realize that you are being judgmental, you have started movement and are on the road to a better solution. Become aware of your body language. When you are "standing firm," with your shoulders squared and your feet planted strongly, you are often standing in judgmental cement. When you hear yourself proving a point or arguing for your position, you are probably defending your own judgmental stance. This may happen either in your conversation or just in your mind as internal dialogue.

Instead of judging, simply witness. To witness is to observe and assess. When you witness, you remain open. Your genuine curiosity allows you to notice more because you are coming from a neutral place. Your thoughts and emotions are still present, but they do not rule your actions. You are able to live in the moment. If you keep thinking about the results you usually get, you will create the reality of your old expectations. Only by suspending judgment and simply witnessing will you open yourself to the larger possibilities of manifesting moment to moment.

Consider two images: First imagine a clamp, such as a woodworker would use to hold two pieces of wood that have been glued together. The job of the clamp is to guarantee immobility so that the two pieces can become cemented. The second image to consider is a flowing stream. The water seems to be gurgling, "ease and flow, ease and flow." Use this next exercise to move toward that stream.

⚔ Claim It! Ease and Flow ⚓

1. As you interact with others today, analyze your body stance, your verbal communication, and your internal dialogue. Are you clamping down, cementing your stance? Or are you experiencing ease and flow, open to accepting new ideas and viewpoints?

2. Which experience is more beneficial?

3. Do you see how fear can motivate you to take a more rigid, clamp-like attitude?

4. As you enter into any situation, hear yourself repeating the mantra "ease and flow, ease and flow."

By making a conscious effort to approach life with ease and flow, you will allow creativity and inspiration to manifest all the answers you need. The answer you seek is never where you have been; if you remain cemented in the past, there can be no break-through and no manifesting of something new. You will also be modeling an ease and flow behavior to others, and empowering them to respond with the same grace. This is exactly what Carrol experienced during a concert tour.

CARROL'S STORY

It was a clear summer evening as I, along with 17 of my students from the University of Arizona, sat onstage at the 2010 World Expo in Shanghai, China. My place was at the very front of the outdoor stage in the center of the Expo grounds. The experience was both exhilarating and frightening: The audience was huge, the spotlights bright, and two video screens behind the group were showing close-ups of us performing. Television cameras were everywhere.

The pressure to perform perfectly was enormous. Even though we had prepared for months, I was experiencing much the same sensations a trained athlete might feel dealing with the anxiety and pressure of the Olympic Games. As I started the concert, I felt tension in my whole body. I started to make some small mistakes and immediately heard negative internal dialogue. *Don't make a mistake!* my mind screamed. My breathing was shallow, and the Kinesthetic sensation of stage fright threatened to overwhelm me.

Because of my training, I knew I could overcome the rising anxiety by redirecting my attention. I started to concentrate on the visual aspects of the performance, not only seeing the harp strings clearly but also envisioning each of the notes of my music. Immediately, my experience shifted from fright to excitement and even enthusiasm.

In this state of acute awareness, I had a powerful revelation—in front of thousands of people! When I viewed the next note in my music as an adversary, a challenge, or a problem, I often made a mistake. If, instead, I welcomed the upcoming note as my friend and opened myself up to it without judgment or fear, my energy flowed around the note and through it, and I experienced joyful achievement.

A few moments after I made this shift in my approach, I felt the energy of the whole ensemble change as everyone adopted my confidence and experienced the joy of expression. As the performance concluded, we all bowed to thunderous applause as the audience rose to their feet in celebration.

Since returning from that trip, Carrol has found that this technique is useful in many situations. Greeting the next moment with ease and flow, as if welcoming a well-known friend, is equally effective in business discussions and interpersonal interactions. As you welcome any situation without fear and visualize success, you allow your creativity and enthusiasm to be present. You are manifesting moment to moment: The past is irrelevant; all that counts is the moment you are greeting now.

Energy flow is a foundation for manifestation. It is also a foundation for good health and vibrant living. Athletes understand that movement allows the body to rebalance and revitalize, clearing stress and depression. Vibrant living, which includes excellent health, requires you to constantly renew and reinvent yourself; the human body completely renews each of its component cells every seven years. To be alive at every level means to open your other dimensions—emotional, mental, heart, and spiritual—to the same constant revitalization. This flow of energy brings you into harmony with your soul and helps you to manifest what you want, moment to moment. Every breath brings a new opportunity.

What gives you life? What maximizes the flow of energy and helps you achieve the most potent manifestation, in tune with your essence and enabling you to use your gifts to achieve your soul mission? Let's look again at how the perspective of five bodies can contribute.

⊰ Claim It! Be Alive, Aware, and Awake! ⊱

1. Sit comfortably in a quiet place where you won't be disturbed as you imagine the vibration of each of these experiences.

2. At the *physical level,* what gives you energy and aliveness? (Walking, being in nature, listening to music, cooking, conversation, cleaning your home, and so on.) How does that feel? Surround yourself with it.

3. At the *emotional level,* what brings you joy? (Art, friendship, playing games, petting an animal.) Bathe in that experience.

4. At the *mental level,* what creates curiosity within you and what supports your interests? (Reading, studying something new, listening to an audio program by an inspirational speaker, coaching children in sports, and so on.) Invite it into your awareness.

5. At the *heart center,* what opens your heart and brings you bliss, fulfillment, and true happiness? (Expressing gratitude, forgiveness, serving, helping others.) Celebrate that experience.

6. At the *spiritual level,* what gives you serenity and peace? (Meditation, prayer, spiritual gatherings, church.) Allow this sensation to envelop you.

7. Which of the previous elements resonate with you as most uplifting? Write those down in your journal, and make a commitment to incorporate these activities into your life for at least the next 40 days.

Living 360 Degrees

During the many stages of our development, the human experience has shifted dramatically. Our very genetic makeup has changed, and technology has allowed us to alter our environment as well. The woodpile fire that was the center of the cave community and provided for so many of its needs has evolved into the glassed-in, gas-fed fire of the condo, which is mostly decorative.

In early human development, survival itself depended on 360-degree awareness to alert people not only to possible dangers but also to potential sources of food. Over the centuries, we've become more and more linear, focused on goals and to-do lists, moving sequentially from one task to the next. Our sphere of awareness has become focused on about 120 degrees: in other words, what is going on in front of us.

We still have the potential, however, to access the full 360-degree circumference of our environment, providing more information that we can integrate into the balanced and grounded state of being that is necessary for manifesting moment to moment.

Doing so provides a powerful grounding tool similar to what a shaman uses. In many spiritual traditions, the shaman is a practitioner who creates a connection to the spiritual world through nature. Before any ritual, the shaman establishes his connection to the directions of north, south, east, and west. He acknowledges where each direction lies in any environment and honors his relationship to each one.

Vibrational Grounding

We can adapt the shaman's practice to our contemporary lives as a way to access all of the energy in our environment. In fact, it is essential that we do so. When we're not grounded, we may be engaged in one task and thinking about something else, without paying attention to what we are doing. We may be driving to work, for example, without being truly present behind the wheel on the busy highway. You can probably think of many similar examples from your life when your attention was scattered. In such circumstances, it's impossible to manifest what you truly desire because you are not connected to your inner experience.

Being grounded means being fully in the moment, aware of your experience in all five dimensions: physical, emotional, mental, heart, and spiritual. With so many distractions leading us into the past or pushing us into the future, it is very difficult for anyone to stay grounded. And yet this must be our constant goal. When we are grounded, we are able to receive our experience and accept it. We reconnect to every aspect of our being. When we are present to our experience, we have a chance to manifest what we truly desire.

The next exercise can help you develop your skill in keeping yourself grounded.

⚔ Claim It! Full Circle ☆

1. Find a quiet place, sit comfortably, and take a couple of deep breaths.

2. Where is your awareness at this moment? Certainly you're looking at this book, but are you aware of other things happening around you?

3. Close your eyes and expand your awareness in a clockwise motion—front, right, back, and left—by acknowledging the sounds, smells, and energies that are just outside of the tunnel vision you traditionally use.

4. Feel the expansiveness of your experience. How will this awareness serve you? Having completed the full circle, what do you notice?

Practice expanding your awareness as often as you can. Here's how Jane drew insights from the exercise.

Jane is a very successful high-level executive who typically goes from one meeting to another without taking any time for herself. She is very driven, and each time she thinks about a new project, she becomes extremely impatient to begin and move forward toward its accomplishment. This negatively impacts her joy factor. Outside of work, she has no energy left to enjoy life.

Thinking about one of her new projects, Jane did the 360-degree exercise. With her eyes closed so that she could be more aware of her sensations, she first connected to the front of her body, and she realized how much anxiety she was carrying there. She then connected to the right side of her body and discovered that she was stiff, not asking for help or relying enough on others for that particular project. When she connected to the back of her body she started to question the importance of that project, and a few more ideas came up to enhance its quality. Finally, she connected to the left side of her body and didn't feel much there.

As she came to the end of the circle, she realized that much of the pressure she had experienced for many years was self-created. She now delegates more often and takes time to question the true importance of each project. Because of the immediate insights this exercise presented, she now engages in this process on a regular basis.

Like Jane, you can find new insights into your life—and important new ideas about how to go forward in tune with your soul's essence—by making regular space in your day for this grounding exercise. Like the shaman, connect to north, south, east, and west, opening your awareness to feel the energy of everything that surrounds you. As you do so, you will also become more aware of when you are in harmony with your energy flow and vibrational alignment, and your ability to manifest moment to moment is amplified.

You may also come to see when it's necessary for you to revitalize and reconsider. Too many people go through life in one of two states: full speed or dead stop. They rush forward, scattering their energy among many projects, until they have run out of steam, or as we say, "burned out." There is an alternative to this strategy, and it's called rest.

The Art of Rest

Resting allows you to renew, revitalize, and reinvent yourself. It gives you the power and the potential to more beneficially understand your current reality and to make the changes necessary in your thoughts, emotions, or behavior to manifest what you desire.

Think of resting as a proactive tool, not just a reactive necessity. In other words, don't wait until you're ready to collapse before you rest. Instead, make rest part of your normal routine, a way to both access and refresh your energy. When you truly rest, you release control, which allows you to receive insights that would otherwise go unnoticed. You can then connect to your inner awareness and access your desires, establishing a foundation for manifestation.

Resting is not encouraged in our society. It's considered an activity for the elderly or for people who are recovering from an illness. Most of us rest only when it is too late, when we are already drained or too exhausted to do anything else. It is often the last option when nothing else is available, or it may be considered a mark of weakness. Instead of this paradigm, Tejpal teaches that resting is a necessary opportunity to open up and create.

TEJPAL'S STORY

When I was a consultant to top executives from Paris to Cairo, one of my chief focuses was to help them learn to work less and rest more, to focus on a few things and do them really well. I helped my clients realize that they could do this without compromising their success. One of the hardest things for them as they took on more responsibilities was *not* to work longer but instead to do the minimum with excellence.

In fact, I urged my clients to cut back to only 40 percent of their scheduled workday. Doing less is much more difficult than doing more because we have to make choices. Creating priorities instead of attempting to do everything is a vital leadership skill. At times I've asked leaders to e-mail me "one goal a day"—the most important thing they would attend to that day. The next morning, they had to send me an e-mail letting me know if they did that one thing the previous day and what the next day's priority was.

It turned out that my clients were the most productive and creative when they reduced their schedule to 40 percent. Yes, they cut back on the number of tasks and meetings, but they remained 100 percent engaged in the rest. This allowed time for them to reflect, embrace unexpected situations, and create. Their potential for innovation became much greater.

Whether or not you are a top executive, you can apply this lesson to your life. The first step is to create a time and space when rest is possible. Following Tejpal's guidance, look through your typical daily schedule and, to begin, eliminate one quarter of the tasks. To do this, you may need to ask others to pick up some of your work, but you may also find that, when you consider whether each task is serving your soul mission, some of them turn out to be unnecessary.

Prioritizing, or choosing, is the ability to ascertain what really matters and to be at peace with that decision. It requires using the new skills in this chapter to get in touch with all of your dimensions and modes of thinking and decide whether you can be comfortable with what you must let go of. Over time, increase the number of tasks you eliminate until you reach 40 percent of your current workload.

Too often people will say they want everything but are unable to create anything; their energy is scattered, and they become stuck. Remember that your ultimate goal is to create change, to manifest your truest desires moment to moment. This means you need to break your established rhythm, which will alter your pattern of thinking, allowing for greater creativity and new outcomes.

Once you have freed up some time, the second step is to use it to rest. How often have you rested, not from exhaustion, but from a place of joy? This exercise can help.

⚮ Claim It! The Rest of the Story . . . ⚮

1. Find a quiet place where you will be undisturbed, and take a couple of deep breaths.

2. Now take an inventory of your five dimensions. What aspect of you needs to rest the most: The physical part? The emotional part? The mental part? The spiritual part? Your heart?

3. What things are restful for you? There are many ways to feed your soul and use your creativity. Again, think of your five dimensions:

- *Physical:* Lie down or sleep; get a massage.

- *Emotional:* Tap into your creative side, drawing, painting, listening to music or playing it.

- *Mental:* Decide to be silent for an hour, quieting your internal thoughts, too.

- *Heart:* Turn to nature for a walking meditation, watching the clouds go by, listening to the rain.

- *Spiritual:* For centuries, chanting and singing have been a way to access the soul's essence, or you may find solace in reading spiritual writing.

4. Choose a mode of rest that suits the dimension most in need of rest. As you repeat this exercise, you may choose a different form of rest each time, depending on the needs of all five bodies or dimensions.

Although it may at first seem counterintuitive, rest is an essential part of staying energized. Attending to the needs of all five dimensions will help you stay aligned so that the flow of energy through your body can reach its maximum.

Unstoppable _You!_

In this chapter, the goal has been to expand your energy resources as much as possible. The vibrancy of your life force is directly connected to your potential to manifest. Through the ideas and exercises here, you can turn away from the negative forces of the past and open your arms to a Universe that loves and supports you in your quest for what you truly desire.

Every day you can find opportunities for celebration and gratitude for "what is" and—most important—"what might be"! Cultivate an attitude of expectancy, anticipating that something amazing and wonderful is waiting just around the next corner. But put aside the judge who would decide what that something must look like. Open yourself up and welcome the mission your soul was born to achieve. Your next phone call may offer you an opportunity more fabulous than anything you could think of.

While you wait, it is important for you to set the stage. If you were inviting guests into your home, you would clean and prepare for their visit. Similarly, when inviting manifestation into your life, it is important to clear your space and your mind to allow unlimited possibilities. The breathing exercise that ends this chapter takes you one more step toward manifestation.

⋇ Claim It! Instant Battery Charge ⋇

1. Find a quiet place where you can be undisturbed.

2. Breathe in through your nose in four segments or steps, with four distinct inhalations. Inhale as deeply into your lower belly as you can, as this will serve to ground and center you.

3. Breathe out through your nose in four segments, pulling in your navel to force the air out.

4. Continue to breathe in this style for three minutes.

5. Quietly imagine a scene in your mind that brings you great joy. It might be a place you have been, or a sunset or a flower. Concentrate quietly on that image.

6. Notice the changes in your body.

This breath and visualization exercise can be done in any environment, even when walking between appointments or waiting to meet someone. Use it to "reboot" your energy and to come into alignment. This combination of intentional breath and personally uplifting image is always available to you to clear, balance, and energize your vibrational flow. We'll tell you more about this process in the coming chapters.

Meanwhile, remember, the only thing that can either stand in your way or open the door to manifestation is *you*. Nurture and embrace your potential in every moment and with every breath.

Intuition Is the Magic Wand

CARROL'S STORY

One afternoon, I was calmly washing dishes in my kitchen in Tucson when I was suddenly hit with the strong sensation that my mother, who was traveling in Canada, had been in a serious car accident. I trusted this intuitive insight and immediately got on the phone to my mother's brother in Alberta, Canada, who completely dismissed my concerns.

But I *knew* something had happened, and I began to call the hospitals in the area where my mother had been traveling. At the second hospital I called, an emergency nurse told me, "Oh, yes, Ida McLaughlin was just brought in."

During this entire episode, there was never a moment's doubt in my mind that my intuition was correct. Once I knew that my mother was receiving care and that the emergency was over, my intuition told me that everything would be fine, which turned out to be exactly the case.

Carrol's "knowing" happened over several thousand miles. As you can see, intuition is not limited by boundaries of distance, time, or space. And the power of intuition belongs to everyone, including you. Think back to when you "knew" something from deep within. Perhaps you had a thought about a friend or family member and at that very moment he or she phoned you. Or you might have noticed a car beside you on the highway and thought, *There's something wrong here. I'll go into the farthest lane away from that car,* only to find that several miles down the road that car was involved in an accident.

A posteriori knowledge—knowledge based on experience or discovery that translates into quantifiable truths—is readily accessible. However, for you to manifest at your highest potential, factual information can't be your only source of knowledge. You need to set aside rational, analytical thinking—the detective part of your mind—and explore what you can learn through your intuitive side. Instead of basing your assessment on logic or fact, simply access the knowing that is inside you. Open yourself to leaps of faith, leaps of trust.

TEJPAL'S STORY

I teach a class in which I help people to develop their intuition. During one exercise, participants work in pairs. They exchange personal objects, then close their eyes and receive the information available through their intuition. The purpose is to see what each person can access about the other through that person's object.

In one of my classes, Mark and Sue were working together. Sue gave Mark what looked like a wedding ring. Mark closed his eyes and first assumed that the ring would bring joyful memories to Sue. He then realized that he might have assumed too much based on his logical thinking. He took a deep breath and relaxed, opening up to his intuition. He felt a profound sadness and saw an image of an older woman. When he shared his intuitive feedback, Sue told him that this ring had belonged to her mother who had passed away six months earlier.

Mark was able to let go of his "detective mind" and open up his senses to a different level of reality. You can do that, too.

Intuition vs. Knowledge

Intuition is a way of receiving information that taps into levels of knowing beyond your physical reality. It requires you to be present and aware, open and receptive, to all of your experiences from moment to moment. In the previous chapter on energy, we saw how exploring all five dimensions—physical, emotional, mental, heart, and spiritual—expands the range of information available to us. We also learned how to tap into Kinesthetic, Visual, and Auditory channels and open our experience to a 360-degree view of our environment.

Like these other tools, intuition is a part of all of us. It is available to us at any time. Like any skill, the more you use your intuition, the easier it becomes to access it, to rely on it and feel confident in the information you receive. Your intuitive powers are stronger than you think. Prove that to yourself by doing the following exercise.

⋅≼ Claim It! Easy Access ≽⋅

1. Look at a person you pass on the street.

2. What does your intuition tell you about them? Are they happy or sad? Are they feeling confident, or are they defeated?

> 3. Do you feel attracted to spend time with them, or are you receiving a warning that you need to stay away?
>
> 4. Does their energy make you feel joyful and cause you to smile, or are you distressed when you witness their despair?

You can use this exercise many times in your day-to-day life. Then, expand your scope. Think of an acquaintance. What information do you intuitively know about this person? Appreciate the great amount of information available to you on a moment-to-moment basis.

To accomplish the results we want in life, we often engage our willpower and our mind. However, as you work on developing your intuition, your will and your mind can actually play against you. Let's explore the distinction between using your intuition and using your will.

Intuition vs. Will

If you traditionally succeed by using your will, you may experience success on one plane but at the same time feel unfulfilled and empty inside. When you're using only your will, you're not living and making decisions guided by what your soul truly desires. In fact, your will creates blind spots and actually limits you. You use your energy to "push through at any price," which means you cannot be aware of anything outside of yourself because of this extreme focus. Opportunities that you might see by broadening your sources of information are closed off to you. You are inflexible, and your intuition is shut down.

Intuition is a very important skill to develop if you want to enhance your ability to manifest moment to moment. Manifestation is a process that requires us to be aware and sensitive to the many sources of information and realities available to us, some on the physical level and others on the spiritual plane. Manifestation embraces both the physical and spiritual dimensions. When we utilize the guidance and signs available to us through our intuition, we are able to create in this physical reality the life we truly desire, thus moment-to-moment manifestation occurs. As you learn to enhance your sensitivity and listen to the subtle messages from your surroundings and your body, you'll discover that it's no longer necessary to use your will or to force things to get the results you want.

Seven Elements of Intuition

No university teaches a curriculum of "Intuition 101." Yet, it is like any skill. While we all have intuition, we can develop it to be stronger and more present in our lives. Exploring and practicing these seven elements of intuition will support you in developing your intuitive skills.

1. Be Clueless!

When you have a problem in your life, there is a tendency to call on an expert to fix the situation. Whether this is related to health, finances, or relationships, the urge to rely on outside solutions is pervasive. Experts are helpful but cannot be your only resource to overcome the challenges you've been presented.

In most cases when you are faced with a problem, you experience tension and anxiety, and your mind jumps ahead into the future. Your thoughts start racing, selecting information to make a decision or to feel reassured. There is a tendency to latch onto one train of thought, and you lose your universal view. Instead of reaching out for more knowledge, accept knowing nothing—just for the moment. Allow yourself to be clueless! When you choose to be clueless, you choose to put your logical mind on the back burner and bring forward every other aspect of your experience, including the physical, emotional, heart, and spiritual. Drop any preconceived ideas, and listen to the intelligence coming from inside you.

Dive into your senses. How does your body feel about the situation? Do you feel pressure in your chest or butterflies in your stomach? Are your shoulders and muscles tense and ready for fight or flight? How are you breathing?

Do you experience any emotions or visualize any images? Be naïve and open to what exists at this moment. When your mind is no longer in the lead, you can reestablish the balance between your mind, body, and spirit. You are immediately able to think "outside the box" and process in a different way than is your habit. You allow yourself to open up to new and different possibilities.

TEJPAL'S STORY

When Mary came to see me, she had been experiencing a lack of energy for quite a while. She'd seen many experts about it and never gotten a satisfying answer.

During the first session, I helped Mary shift the relationship she had with her condition. Instead of looking for a definitive answer, I asked her to relax and connect to her problem, to make contact with the place of disease and stay there—without preconceived ideas.

Being clueless, she started to get new insights and realized she had never processed some painful situations with her mother, who had passed away seven years earlier. As she started to release these painful emotions, her energy started to rise. She shifted her relationship with her disease and opened the door for further healing.

As you see from Mary's story, being clueless is not forever. The idea is to pause—just pause for a few precious moments—and allow yourself to be completely open and stay curious. Instead of trying to jump in with a solution, relax and empty your mind. Allow yourself to receive the messages from your intuition.

TEJPAL'S STORY

In my practice, clients often come to me burdened with the following questions regarding their health, relationships, or work challenges: "What does it mean?" "What do you know about my disease?" "Do I need to quit my job?" Often, my first answer is, "I don't know."

This simple answer allows me to create inner stillness, to pause, to change my breath and experience the situation with all my senses. This allows space and time for my intuition to guide me.

You may wish to use Tejpal's technique yourself. When you allow yourself to "not know," then often your relationship with the problem shifts, and you open the door for intuitive answers to arise. Following is an exercise that uses your imagination to help you see the value of being clueless.

⤜ Claim It! If I Were an Animal . . . ⤞

1. Find a quiet place where you won't be disturbed, and practice your breathing until you are calm and fully present in the moment.

2. Select an animal that attracts or inspires you, and pretend you are this animal.

3. Imagine you're in its skin, feeling its movements and experiencing the world through its perception.

4. Now move around the room as if you were this animal. Make its sounds; view the world from its vantage point.

5. Next, choose a challenge in your life where you would like to gain some insight. It could be how to handle a specific situation, how to understand what a particular person is feeling, or even what to do during your next day off.

6. Experience these questions through the essence of the animal you have chosen—from the animal's point of view. How does this animal respond? What insights have you gained?

The answers you find don't need to be logical or make complete sense—in fact, logic is exactly where we don't want to go. The exercise is meant to help you break out of your habitual way of thinking and feeling so that you can discover a new way to interpret and access information. The more you engage in viewing through an alternate way and quiet the logical, thinking mind, the easier it gets and the more open you are to hearing your own intuitive voice.

2. Be Detached

Detachment means accepting exactly what exists at any given moment. We've all heard of the advantages of letting go, not holding on to the past, and detaching, but it is difficult to do. There is a general perception that being detached means not having emotions, not having feelings about events or people who come and go in your life. If that's what it meant—a life without joy, sadness, or enthusiasm—it's no wonder people don't want to detach!

That's not it, though. Being detached doesn't exclude having a wide range of emotions and perhaps even judgments. Rather, we need to recognize and acknowledge our emotional reactions and feelings but keep them from becoming the guiding force behind our actions and thoughts. People think that if they deny or stuff their emotions, it will diminish the emotions' power. In fact, trying to suppress emotions simply gives them the fuel to take over your life and drive your behavior. Only by acknowledging your emotional truth and giving it a voice can you "take the wind out of the sail" and become able to consciously choose what to do.

We tend to think about practicing detachment only when it concerns something negative and rarely consider it necessary when it concerns something positive. In fact, you will benefit by practicing detachment about everything. Each time you hold on to something you have experienced in the past, you block yourself from being open to the present. For example, you had a great vacation, and you want the next one to be exactly the same. This restricts the potential for an even better experience by creating preconceived expectations. Detachment allows you to be in the moment, which is an important component of developing your intuition to its full potential.

When it comes to intuition, you must detach from expectations not only about outcome, but also about how you will receive information when accessing your intuition. Realize that you may experience your intuition in any number of forms, such as seeing, hearing, and feeling. You never know how the information you want might present itself. The strongest and clearest messages sometimes come as big surprises, as participants in Tejpal and Carrol's intuition class have found.

TEJPAL AND CARROL'S STORY

In our intuition classes, people who access their intuition have powerful experiences that take them by surprise.

For example, Tania worked with Linda: "When I held her glasses, I didn't know what to do," Tania recalls. "My mind started to wander, and I thought that Linda was shy and quiet. Suddenly, inside my head, I heard her laughing really hard. I was truly taken by surprise. It was so strong, I knew it was real."

With intuition, you never know what you're going to get or how it will come. You're not even sure you will understand the message right away. You need to switch from being a detective and trying to figure things out to being an intuitive. You must trust instead of judging whether it's right or wrong. Stay relaxed and remain open to accepting different kinds of information. Here's what happened to Vicki when she followed this advice:

Vicki sat next to a woman in her 50s, well dressed and appearing very strong. When she received the woman's object, a watch, she expected to intuit something in harmony with that image. Vicki was amazed when she saw in her mind's eye a quickly flowing river with rapids and waterfalls. She allowed herself to flow with the image, and saw that after the rapids there was a calm, restful lake that seemed very serene.

Vicki followed the instructions and didn't put any particular "story" to her intuitive experience; she simply shared it with the woman. To her great surprise, the woman was visibly affected by the story. She told Vicki it represented exactly what she was experiencing in her life: a great deal of trauma and change. Her strongest desire was that she would find some peace, and hearing about the restful lake, she felt much calmer.

Sometimes an issue such as the loss of a job, quarrels with a partner or child, or disagreements with your boss can feel so overwhelming that it seems to color everything in your life. When an issue becomes so prominent, we think of it as being "hooked"—like a fish on a line. The hook can often follow a theme: worry about money, lack of self-confidence, fear of failure. It influences every experience. Being hooked is the opposite of being detached. When we're hooked, our mind and emotions are frozen into a pattern that will prevent our intuition from flowing.

Lisa has always yearned to be recognized and loved by her mother. They live in different countries, so they see each other only once a year. Each time Lisa goes to visit her mother, she brings many presents, as well as money to help her mother financially. Her mother never says thank you, and never asks how Lisa is doing or what's happening in her life. Each time, Lisa comes home devastated. She is unable to accept her mother's behavior and keeps hoping that before her mother dies, she will recognize all Lisa has done for her. Lisa is hooked into this unlikely scenario.

Here's an exercise that can help you detach from thoughts or feelings that have a particularly powerful hold on you.

⊰ Claim It! Unhook ⊱

1. Find a quiet place where you won't be disturbed, and practice your breathing until you are calm and fully present in the moment.

2. Think of something in your life that really has you "hooked"; something that you are attached to, that throws you into a state of turmoil. It may involve a member of your family whose love and acceptance is so important to you that it influences all of your decisions and actions. Or perhaps it's about your son choosing a college, or your boss's behavior.

3. Visualize this hook in a glass ball that you are holding above your head.

4. Take a moment to look at the picture you've created! You are walking around in your life, trying to be successful, but one of your arms is unusable because you're carrying your glass ball that contains "the hook."

5. Now imagine that the glass ball can float in the air by itself. It is free to move. It can still be part of your life, but not at your personal expense. You can let it go!

6. Once you've let go, you have detached. Feel the freedom of not supporting the weight of your hook.

By letting go of your hook, you have detached and are now more open and able to access your intuition to a much greater degree. And, there's an additional benefit: In this scenario, everyone wins. If there are people involved in your hook, you have given them power to move in ways that weren't possible when you were hooked in, holding up the ball.

3. Be Grounded

As we saw in the Energy chapter, being grounded is being connected to the earth, feeling balanced, focused, and at one with nature and the Universe. The more grounded you are, the easier it is to access your intuition and receive relevant information.

If you're tired, worried about something, or in pain, it will be extremely difficult to ground and access your intuition. You will most likely go into fear or negativity and shut down any possibility to receive intuitively. When the physical body is fully alive and full of energy at the cellular level, then it becomes much easier to call on your spiritual body and access your intuition.

Each of us has a unique way of being grounded, and we encourage you to experiment and find what serves you best. Many of the breathing exercises presented in this book are excellent grounding tools. Physical exercise also helps—walking barefoot on the earth, practicing yoga, performing a walking meditation (described later in this chapter). When you move your body with presence and intention, you are less subject to your negative thought patterns, and it's easier to connect, not only with the physical, but also with emotional, heart, and spiritual dimensions.

Another tool is to visualize yourself connected to the energy of the earth, as we do in this next exercise.

> ### ⟨ Claim It! Your Tree of Life ⟩
>
> 1. Find a quiet place where you won't be disturbed, and practice your breathing until you are calm and fully present in the moment.
>
> 2. Stand with your feet hip-width apart.
>
> 3. Visualize a beautiful, tall tree somewhere in nature. Become this tree. Let your spine represent the trunk. Feel the roots of your tree extending down your legs through the soles of your feet and deep into the earth.
>
> 4. As you become the tree, inhale deeply. Hold the breath in, then exhale to let go and renew. Repeat this cycle for three minutes.
>
> 5. As you do so, feel the energy of the earth coming up through your feet and legs, up through your spine, and into every part of your body.

From this place of relaxed integration, you have a foundation that will allow your intuition to be received. As you become one with the earth, you experience a sense of wholeness that facilitates intuition.

4. Trust Yourself

To access your intuition, you simply need to trust yourself and listen to the insights that come to you. You don't need to have any special knowledge. If you haven't been accessing your intuition, you may find it difficult at first to believe the messages it is sending you. It may take some time to develop this trust, but the outcome is worth the effort.

As you explore and learn to trust the messages you receive from your intuition, you may want to start with less important issues to build your confidence. The following exercise helps to build a foundation for you to rely on as you seek the knowledge within.

⁛⟨ Claim It! Launch Your Intuition ⟩⁛

1. Block your right nostril with your right thumb or finger. Inhale through the left nostril for a count of five. Hold the breath in for a count of five. Exhale through the left nostril for a count of five, and hold the breath out for the same count.

2. Breathing through the left nostril activates the right brain, which is the creative, intuitive brain. Repeat this pattern a minimum of five times.

3. Close your eyes and become aware of all your senses. Hear all the sounds around you. Feel your breath enter your lungs, and envision yourself in a place where you feel peaceful.

4. Notice what comes to you. Don't analyze or question anything; just accept your experience in the moment.

5. Take a deep breath and hold it in for ten seconds or more. Be grateful for what you have received.

Begin practicing this a few minutes at a time. The information is always there, and you can access it in a split second. Don't allow too much time—too much time fosters rational, linear thinking.

Even so, as you start exploring your intuition, you may wonder if you are making things up, if what you access is "real." This self-questioning comes from the rational mind, and it can easily become an obstacle to receiving information from the part of you that is all-knowing. Acknowledge any negative thoughts, worries, or doubts that you hear as chatter in your mind. Then reduce the power of the doubts and tensions that inhibit the free flow of information by simply accepting what your intuition tells you. Trust that every image, word, or feeling from your intuition carries valuable insights.

When the two of us teach our intuition course together, we often begin with the premise: "Pretend you are always right." By holding that thought, you leave no space for doubt, fear, or worry. You trust every aspect of your intuition, even when it doesn't make sense to you. This position of acceptance and nonlinear thinking opens the gate for manifestation. You are accepting like a sponge.

5. Be a Sponge

Receiving is an important element of intuition. Try considering yourself as a sponge. A sponge absorbs everything. It simply receives without organizing or processing in any way. In contrast, our minds love to label, classify, and organize. Without conscious awareness, our minds constantly filter all of the information that we receive. As a result of this we judge, distrust, and create walls. For example, when we receive something good, we might question what we'll have to give back in the future and whether or not we are worthy.

To get the most from our intuition, it is helpful to understand that there is no such thing as important or unimportant information. Everything has value. For intuition to come to us, we must be ready to receive everything, to act like a sponge. Allow yourself to gratefully accept even more than you can imagine. The following exercise shows you how to perform a walking meditation, which integrates both grounding and sponging. It can be easily incorporated into your day.

⅍ Claim It! Sponging ⅋

1. As you take four steps, breathe in through your nose.

2. On each step, repeat to yourself one syllable of a mantra or other phrase that is meaningful to you. You may choose something like the mantra "Sa-Ta-Na-Ma," which comes from Sanskrit and means "infinity, life, death, rebirth,"[1] or the phrase "A-maz-ing Grace."

3. On the next four steps, exhale through your nose, again repeating that mantra in your mind.

4. Continue for ten minutes. By coordinating your breath, steps, and mantra, you create synchronicity and unify your mind, body, and spirit.

5. Choose a quiet place to sit. Close your eyes and listen, sponging in all the sounds you can hear. Do you hear the wind, traffic, birds, or human voices? You will most likely be able to hear more than ten sounds.

6. Absorb this symphony of sound as you extend your awareness and allow your intuition to blossom.

As you do this exercise, try not to be selective or analytical. What you understand is less important than your openness to the environment around you. By accepting what you hear, see, and feel, you will become more open to the messages your intuition is giving you.

6. Be Playful

How often do you let yourself play? Do you even remember how? Do you value pleasure? Do you know how to relax and express your joyfulness? In our serious, achievement-oriented culture, too many people leave play behind with childhood.

The more playful and alive you are, the more open you are to new possibilities. Playfulness engages your physical body as well as your mind and your spirit, and you are open to receive and accept any intuitive information that comes to you. A playful spirit and attitude helps you accept what is happening in your life and be flexible when necessary. Playfulness helps you make decisions from your intuitive self and thus facilitates manifestation of what is truly aligned with your soul mission.

How Do You Like to Play?

Bring playfulness into your life. Depending on your unique personality and how you are designed energetically, there are various ways to experience playfulness. Here are some possibilities. Which persona are you?

- *The Creator:* You love expressing yourself through any form of art. When you create, you feel like your whole being is engaged and energized. You become spontaneous in your expression and that gives you great joy.

- *The Adventurer:* You like exploring and trying new things. Your curiosity makes you alive and vibrant.

- *The Challenger:* You love being challenged either through your physical body or your mind. Competing physically in anything or being engaged in strategic games is really fun for you.

There are many other possibilities. What style is yours? How can you bring more playfulness into your life?

Play is one of the fastest ways to relax. When we are playful, we learn to be relaxed and alert at the same time. Often people associate being relaxed with falling asleep or "zoning out," or else they are alert and tense, focusing on a to-do list, a goal to achieve, or a problem to solve. Playfulness offers the opportunity to experience relaxation and alertness simultaneously. When you hold both states at the same time, your intuition will increase tremendously.

Play is so important that we recommend including it when planning your schedule until making time to play becomes a natural part of your routine. The following exercise will help.

⋅≼ Claim It! Playtime ≽⋅

Before you start your day, take a moment to consider what your schedule looks like.

- How much time are you dedicating to play?

- Have you already filled every available moment with a "should do" list?

- What can you do to include more playfulness in your day?

- What style did you resonate most with: the Creator, the Adventurer, or the Challenger? How can that persona be a part of your day?

7. Be Nurturing

To develop your intuition, you need to be rested and balanced. If you're physically exhausted or experiencing a difficult time in your life, it can be much more challenging to open yourself up to your intuition. These are the times that it becomes key to nurture yourself, rest, and heal. Self-care exists on several levels. First there is traditional self-care on the physical level with rest, nutrition, and fitness. Equally as important is your spiritual and emotional self-care. This next exercise will make sure that you attend to all the dimensions of your being when it's time to take care of yourself.

⋅⟨ Claim It! Nurture Yourself ⟩⋅

1. Find a quiet place where you won't be disturbed, and practice your breathing until you are calm and fully present in the moment.

2. Begin by considering **the space** where you spend most of your time.

- Do the colors of your walls, rugs, and furniture please you? How about the lighting?

- Do you have open, uncluttered spaces?

- What view do you have? Can you see nature? Do you have a garden or indoor plants?

- Do you have a space for art and creativity?

3. Now think about your **relationships.**

- Are some of your relationships toxic or depressing to you?

- If necessary, clear the air with family and friends so there is room for open and honest communication.

- Do you need personal time alone? Are you getting enough?

- Do you share time with uplifting, inspiring people? Those who share common loves (yoga, music, golf)?

- If not, think about how you can connect with people like that.

4. Take a deep breath and explore your **personal rhythm.**

- What is your most effective time—morning, midday, or evening? Do you take advantage of your personal biorhythm?

- How much sleep do you need? Would a daily nap help?

- Are you always in a hurry?

5. Consider your **self-image.**

- How do you feel about your body image? Does it please you or pull you down?

- Do you pay attention to how you dress? There is energy in clothing and personal presentation that can be very uplifting. Remember your joy factor as you choose your clothes for the day.

6. Finally, look at how your life honors **the sacred.**

- Do you take time to meditate each day? Do you take time to be grateful?

- Do you have a sacred haven in your home where you go to rejuvenate and rest?

- Are you honoring your life purpose, your soul mission?

- What do you do that makes you smile?

- Do you establish a clear intent before starting any activity?

Now that you have tools to develop your intuition, we invite you to practice them on a regular basis. Pick one of the seven elements explored in this chapter, and practice the corresponding Claim It! for at least ten days in a row. Which one serves you the most? Use your intuition to decide!

Like an athlete who must create a lifestyle to support his or her passion, create a lifestyle that empowers you to be at your best—open, aware, and relaxed. As you learn to rely more and more on your intuition, you will know when to speed up, slow down, or put things aside for the moment. You will become part of the natural flow of moment-to-moment manifestation where great things are accomplished with little effort.

The flexibility and insights gained by using your intuition will also make it much easier to shift and become unstuck from limiting beliefs or other aspects of your personal story that are hindering your manifestation—the subject of our next chapter.

YOUR BELIEF AND YOUR STORY DO NOT DEFINE YOU AND CAN BE CHANGED

What we tell ourselves about our lives has a tremendous influence on what we feel worthy of and capable of manifesting. There are two elements that form the basis of how we view ourselves and our lives. These are our story and our belief. In this chapter, we'll explore the hidden power of these two concepts; both beliefs and stories can be changed to better your life and multiply your potential to manifest.

Your *story* consists of your history, your childhood, your successes, and your challenges in life. It is always with you. It constitutes a living part of your reality. Yet in truth, your story gives only a partial picture of your identity. Since your story is based in the past, it is a frozen image. Rewriting your story allows it to flow and opens the door to greater possibilities for transformation and manifestation in the present and future.

Belief is something you've created based on your assumptions and experience. It is a product of environment, learning, experience, lineage, and myriad other stimuli, many of which you don't even consciously remember. While belief can sometimes be very clear, it also can sometimes be unknown, mysterious, and hidden.

It is helpful to make the distinction between your story and your belief. Your story is what you think happened to you and how you describe your life experience. A belief is a statement that summarizes your feelings and interpretation of different aspects of your life. For example, your story might be that from an early age, your family was stressed about money and never felt that there was enough. Your belief on that subject today might be that you will never have enough money and that you have to be very restricted with how you spend it. Your stories and beliefs are intertwined yet independent, and may sometimes be difficult to separate.

Originating as far back as your childhood, your story often lacks nuances and seldom represents the whole picture. Some people may formulate a story about themselves that emphasizes one or more dramatic events that they experienced. Others might block those same experiences from their consciousness. Whether your personal story is full of uplifting images or devastating remembrances, it will dramatically impact your life. The more attached you are to your story and think that it is the truth, the stronger its impact upon you. This will, in turn, affect your ability to develop to your full potential and reinvent yourself.

Erin was an accountant who worked in her family's business. She struggled with her body image and, in the last five years, had put on over 100 pounds. In her work, Erin found herself not completing assignments and arriving as much as one hour late for important meetings. She kept hearing herself say, *I am stupid. I should be able to do this.* When asked during a healing session where those statements originated, Erin broke into tears and recalled her mother saying many times that she was "stupid and selfish."

Erin was able to realize how her feelings of not being good enough in her mother's eyes resulted in her forming self-sabotaging habits in many areas of her life. When Erin understood that she didn't have to continue to be affected by that story, she chose to alter her beliefs, and her life began to change.

Realizing that your story is not the absolute truth can be an empowering shift toward self-discovery. Much can be learned by examining, and sometimes altering, the story you believe about yourself.

Your Story Is Not Who You Are

The mind often craves safety and security. Therefore, it will create a story that allows you to cope and feel in control. With that being the case, consider your story simply as one understanding of an experience, one view or interpretation. Problems occur when you believe that you *are* your story and that the story is true, complete, and unchangeable. When this happens, your story takes control of your present reality, as well as your future. Adherence to the story prevents you from being open to new possibilities and welcoming changes in your life. Rather than considering your story to be cemented and stagnant, realize that it can be viewed from a different perspective, which facilitates moment-to-moment manifestation. Consider your story from three different vantages: negative, positive, and neutral.

The negative perspective sees only the dangers, limitations, and failures that could result from an idea or situation. The positive perspective focuses on what is good about the idea or situation and what positive outcomes can be gained from it. The neutral perspective can embrace all the limitations and potential of both the positive and negative but isn't attached to either viewpoint. In many ways, the neutral perspective can offer the most beneficial information because it synthesizes all aspects of the situation and allows you to detach from stories and beliefs that may hold you back. Let's look at Judith's life:

Here are the basics of Judith's story:

- I am the eldest child of six.
- My mother had a weak immune system and was very often sick.
- My dad traveled a lot for work.

From these simple facts, Judith could weave a number of different stories of her life:

- **From a negative perspective,** Judith might say that she had to raise her siblings and therefore never had time for herself.
- **From a positive perspective,** Judith could say that she felt appreciated and valued by the other five children and was able to be an important influence in their lives.
- **From a neutral perspective,** Judith learned to be responsible and developed leadership skills.

Take a look at your own life and realize that you have the ability to expand your experience by viewing it from different perspectives.

⊰ Claim It! What's Your Story ⊱

1. In your journal, write three to five sentences reflecting the basic facts about your life, just as Judith did. Make sure that no opinions creep in; "I was the youngest child" is a fact; "I was the prettiest child" might be a matter of opinion.

2. View each statement from a negative perspective (what was painful).

3. Now explore your sentences from a positive perspective (what brought you joy).

4. Finally, look at your story from a neutral perspective (detached).

5. Go back to the original sentences you wrote about your life. By viewing each sentence from the perspective listed above, do you experience your story differently?

The Kaleidoscope of Your Reality

Sir David Brewster first invented the kaleidoscope in 1816. The name *kaleidoscope* is derived from the Greek *kalos,* which means beautiful; *eidos,* which means shape; and *skopeo,* which means to look at, to examine, or to observe. The beauty of viewing objects through a kaleidoscope is that when the tube is rotated, the colored objects inside are reflected by numerous mirrors, presenting the viewer with a dazzling display of colors and patterns. The colored objects don't change, but they appear different as the kaleidoscope turns and the objects are viewed from alternative perspectives. Each rotation presents a very different visual reality.

It is extremely telling to examine your life as if you were viewing it through a kaleidoscope.

·⟨ Claim It! Picture Your Life ⟩·

1. As a starting place, imagine eight to ten pieces of colored glass. Each piece of glass represents an element of your life. You may imagine a relationship between a color of glass, such as fuchsia, and a thought, such as your joy factor and playfulness. Similarly, the size of an imagined piece, such as a small piece, might indicate a timid or less visible aspect of your personality.

2. Name your glass pieces. Write what they represent on a piece of paper for future reflection. For example, your internal kaleidoscope might contain:

- Blue: life balance, health, and self-care

- Red: desire to succeed, your ambition, and career

- Green: your belief in your potential

- Yellow: traditions, values you hold

- Orange: relationships, intimacy

- Fuchsia: fun factor, playfulness

- Brown: relationship with money

- White: external referencing, how you are viewed by others

3. Look through the tube of your imaginary kaleidoscope. By twisting the kaleidoscope, you'll immediately see different parts of yourself rise to the top of the picture, creating a new *eidos,* or shape. This will present a new opportunity for *skopeo,* a way to examine and observe your life.

4. Turn your kaleidoscope and imagine that you are seeing yourself as if through another person's eyes. What you see as lacking might be viewed very differently from another person's perspective. You may feel, *I'm not good enough, I can't do anything right,* whereas another person might view your endeavors as extraordinary.

5. Another turn of the kaleidoscope might present the question, "Have my priorities changed?" You may have strived for years to become the most respected person in your field. Now, having achieved that position, you are bored and restless. Twist your kaleidoscope and view your situation from a perspective of gratitude for having achieved a life dream.

6. As you turn your kaleidoscope further, imagine yourself on holiday in a fabulous place surrounded by people you love. How do you view your life picture from that relaxed perspective? What parts of you become more important? Do you want those parts of yourself to be more present on a day-to-day basis? How can this new realization impact your life?

In the same way that the tiniest turning of a kaleidoscope completely alters what you see, even a small adjustment can open myriad possibilities in how you interpret your current situation and your potential.

Your life is much more than what you first see. There is a wealth of uncovered potential within you awaiting your discovery. Be willing to turn your kaleidoscope. Welcome change and consider "what if." Experience life's constant flow and invite creativity into your reality. Like your story, your beliefs can also affect your possibility to manifest, either propelling you toward or holding you back from achieving what you desire.

Anatomy of Belief

A belief can either uplift you or restrict you. It can be a powerful, positive force or deeply troubling. Any medical practitioner or healer will testify to the importance of a patient's belief toward vibrant health. Breakthroughs happen when patients believe they can be healed and also believe in the power of the healer. In fact, your beliefs define the reality you create.

Uplifting beliefs include:

- "I always bounce back no matter what."

- "I can always ask for and get some help."

- "People love to help."

- "The world is open for new ideas."

Some examples of limiting beliefs are:

- "I have to do everything by myself."

- "Working hard is the only way to be successful."

- "Some people are lucky and have it easy."

- "Nobody understands me."

- "There are no jobs available in these tough economic times."

The following case histories show how people's beliefs impact their ability to manifest:

> Cassandra has been a designer working in a large company for the past 20 years. At this time in her life, she wants more freedom and flexibility and doesn't like the constant pressure she feels from her boss.
>
> Cassandra believes she lives in a world that is extremely abundant and that she can succeed at anything she tries. Holding that belief, she decides to change jobs, leaving the company she's been with and starting her own design business. Cassandra's belief that she will succeed

at anything she tries is an important element in allowing herself to leave the safety of a known job and manifest the future she desires.

Jack believes he can't succeed. He has a menial job waiting tables at a diner and barely makes enough money to support his family. One day, a businessman at the restaurant tells Jack about an opening in his catering business. At first, Jack is excited and wants to try the new job, but the more he thinks about it, the more reasons he finds that they wouldn't hire him. In the end, he doesn't even apply because of his belief that he will fail.

Seeing the impact of beliefs, you can understand how important it is to examine your own.

Multigenerational Beliefs

Many of your beliefs don't begin with you. They have been handed down for generations, like a blueprint amalgamated from your environment, culture, family traditions, and experience. You are often neither aware of the root nor the implications of your beliefs.

Because of your background, your ethnic heritage, and many other elements, you have an inherited viewpoint through which you process your life. These filters become part of your story, carrying an emotional charge and often including a value judgment on your potential, your worth, and your capability. You cannot overestimate its influence.

What is your personal story, and what are your beliefs? In the following exercise, explore areas of your life from a generational perspective and discover beliefs and thought patterns that have been carried through your family, much like your DNA.

⊰ Claim It! Your Lineage and Your Beliefs ⊱

1. Go through the list below, and answer the questions from your own perspective, writing them down in your manifesting journal.

- *Money:* Is it okay to be rich? Do I deserve it? Do I manage my poverty, or do I manage my abundance?

- *Success/Acknowledgment:* Do I want to be successful? Do I think I deserve it? Do I believe I can be abundant?

- *Self-expression:* Do I think my opinions are worthy of being heard? Do I share my truth, or do I hold back? Am I afraid to be unique?

- *Happiness:* Is happiness really present in my life? Do I make joy a priority? Do I consider myself responsible for the happiness of others? Do I view happiness as my birthright or as something that has to be earned?

- *Health:* Do I value my health and live a lifestyle that supports it? Do I deserve good health? Do I listen to my intuition about what I need?

- *Pleasure and Fun:* Is pleasure a part of my life? Do I believe in the value of pleasure, or do I think of it as a distraction? What have I done for myself that honors my joy factor?

- *Trust:* How do I experience trust? Does it take a long time for me to trust? What needs to be present for me to trust?

2. Now imagine yourself as your mother, then your father, and answer the same questions, using a separate page in your journal for each person.

3. Make sure to process these questions both from your own perspective and that of your parents. As you explore each area, what do you notice? Do you uncover attitudes or stories that are uncomfortable?

4. As you notice these thought patterns, remember that you're capable of altering your beliefs and thus changing the path of your life.

It's Your Choice—Changing Your Beliefs

People often have beliefs that they've carried for years and are not aware of.

The moment you uncover any belief that doesn't serve you, you can begin to reconstruct another reality that better serves your desire. Here's how Jacob did that:

Jacob owned a manufacturing company. He used to go to work at 5 A.M. every day, and he stayed until late at night because he felt he had to check everything himself to ensure it was being done correctly. He saw himself getting more tired and impatient and finally decided to get some help.

Talking with his coach, Jacob realized that his leadership style was based in fear. He didn't think that his team was competent. Jacob had held a belief since early childhood that he had to do everything on his own. When he uncovered that limiting belief, he dramatically changed his management style and let his team have much more responsibility. Because of Jacob's empowering his employees, they began to be more engaged and creative, not just in their specific areas, but in the success of the company as a whole. This allowed Jacob to be more entrepreneurial and to be a visionary regarding the company's future. Jacob now uses his creativity in ways that better serve the advancement of the company.

As you can see, beliefs can be changed. This may involve breaking out of a mold that was perhaps set down by parents, society, or the expectations of others. It's vital to understand that no matter what created your beliefs, they were originally intended to support and assist you. Do not judge your beliefs; rather, simply acknowledge them. View them with compassion instead of criticism. The important thing is to realize that you have the ability to transform, alter, and change any belief so that it can serve you rather than hinder you. You have the power to reconstruct your beliefs to support the manifestations you desire.

Who Is on Your Team?

Some assumptions and belief systems are so alive that they resemble characters. These characters, sometimes hidden from your consciousness, can control your life and prevent you from creating that which you desire. Here are some of the worst offenders:

- **Mr. No You Can't** focuses on the blocks, on the problems, on why something can't work. He sees only the negative and the obstacles.

- **Ms. Perfection** believes that only when everything is perfect will she be able to manifest.

- **Luckless** believes that abundance and desired manifestation are products of luck and don't involve an individual's intentions or hard work.

- **But Wait** never feels ready to manifest, to attract, or to show up and be accountable.

- **Spacey Tracie** is content to just dream, imagine, and never *do* anything.

- **Mini Me** always feels inadequate, incompetent, and unworthy to receive.

- **Scaredy-Cat** wants a guarantee of the results before daring to begin and is very concerned with what will happen if "it" doesn't work.

- **Need D** never has enough time, money, help, or whatever is necessary to succeed, and always feels lacking.

- **Mr. Do Nuthin'** believes "I don't have to do anything or have any responsibility. Things just happen. I'm waiting for it all to work out."

- **He Done It!** believes that it is always someone else's fault. He Done It! accepts no responsibility and therefore isn't willing to learn, to be accountable, or to elevate to a place where manifestation is possible.

Now it's your turn. Use the following exercise to name and create descriptions of your own internal colleagues.

❖ Claim It! He/She Who Must Be Named ❖

1. Relax, close your eyes, and take a few deep breaths.

2. Which of the characters listed above (or their relatives) lives inside you?

3. Have you seen that character operating in the lives of others around you? Perhaps in members of your family?

4. Invite the character to have a conversation with you in your mind.

5. Thank it for being present in your life. Explain that you realize its original purpose was to help you and that you're grateful for the powerful impact it has had.

6. Suggest that now you need to change its role. Ask the character to retool and reshape the way that it serves you. Express what it is you need at this point in your life. Listen to the character's vantage point.

7. Negotiate an agreement on how the character can serve you. Address any objections the character may have about its new functions until you are in agreement about its new role.

8. Agree to check in occasionally and see how everything is working. (Be sure to follow through.)

9. Thank the character and acknowledge the change that you see in your reality.

The work you've done in this exercise is an important foundation for transformation and manifestation. Whereas your internal character was previously operating from a solitary and somewhat hidden place, you have now created a partnership that includes open communication. You have defined a new paradigm for yourself. You and your inner characters are now consciously co-creating your life. Here's how the exercise worked for Laura:

Laura is very energetic and extremely committed in everything she does. She has a high level of expectation and loves things to be perfect, yet she gets disappointed when she realizes that nobody recognizes her outstanding accomplishments.

As she does the exercise, Laura realizes that Ms. Perfection is her strongest character. Because her mother, Lucy, had the same traits, Laura decides to call her character *Lucia*. She thanks Lucia for her outstanding performance and points out that it would be even more perfect if joy were associated with the experience instead of just working hard. Before the start of every project, or at the beginning of each day, Laura asks Lucia what would make the project more joyful, and then she incorporates what Lucia asks. Several times during each project, Laura checks with Lucia to see whether the joy factor is still present or if something needs to be altered to achieve it.

Open and Expand

In Laura's story, we saw how limiting beliefs can be transformed in ways that support the manifestation of our desires. It is also true that some beliefs can be extremely beneficial (or extremely important) in opening you up to new possibilities. Here are three core beliefs that are essential to manifestation:

1. **Abundance.** At the core of the process of manifestation is the understanding that the Universe is extremely abundant. There are no shortages. When you recognize this abundance, you will be uplifted and empowered, as you come to believe in your capabilities to create your deepest desires. Accepting abundance and realizing your worthiness is an empowering experience.

2. **Readiness to Receive.** An important element of attracting manifestation is to be ready to receive. Too often we focus only on asking for what we desire, while we forget the most challenging part of the equation—receiving. The idea of receptivity is often

forgotten. It is easy to be guarded, willing to receive only what we know or understand. For true abundance, however, we must be ready to receive everything. Do this by being open and sensitive, allowing yourself to gratefully accept even more than you can imagine.

Receiving helps you connect to your heart and honor yourself. If you believe that you are not worthy, are not ready, or do not deserve to receive, then you do not allow the possibility of manifestation. In fact, by thinking this way, you're looking for reasons manifestation cannot occur rather than expecting it to happen.

Receiving requires humility and gratitude. Receiving also becomes easier with practice. Your job in the process is to be clear about what you want and be ready to receive it. Then, let the Universe manifest in its own perfect way. You don't have to work out all the details—in fact, that only restricts the flow. Your part is to desire, believe, and receive.

3. **Awareness: Honor the Moment.** Every moment offers a new opportunity, an awakening, a clean slate from which to manifest something new. It marks the start of a new personal story for your life. This moment, right now, is truly all that exists. To expend precious energy being concerned about history or the future is not compatible with creating at your highest level.

As you commit to manifesting what you desire, you must be willing to detach from the past as well as from the future. Concern for what *has* happened or what *might someday* happen locks you into a linear thought pattern. This restricts the creative energy that is inherent in the world of possibility and in every moment.

The Storyboard

Often it's easier to see behavioral patterns in other people than in yourself. When you realize how other people's lives are influenced by their stories and beliefs, it helps you acknowledge the effect your story has upon you and your life. Consider the following examples:

Jeff was a powerful business executive in New York. One year, he experienced a financial crisis and lost virtually everything. Despite this event, Jeff held a core belief that he was an excellent businessman. Because of this internal picture, his setback didn't stop him. His mind-set was positive, and he held a belief that he would be successful. He made decisions and investments that were in harmony with his expectations of success. Five years later, Jeff was again a millionaire.

TEJPAL'S STORY

My parents always believed that the world was not a welcoming place and that every aspect of existence had to be challenging and hard. It took me years to realize that I was also carrying this belief. I was always guarded and vigilant, yet disconnected from my feelings and the amount of fear I was experiencing. When I started working, I was always attracted to the most difficult assignments that had a high level of risk.

With the help of counselors and healers, I discovered that I was holding my parents' beliefs and realized that I didn't have to hang on to them. I started to trust the world more, learned to ask for help, and attracted situations that were more in alignment with my soul mission. From being a driven, demanding leader always asking for more, I was able to develop my ability to listen and receive to help people around the world enhance their lives.

As Tejpal changed her focus and expectations from facing constant challenges to being excited about life's possibilities, her reality also changed.

You, the Story Writer

There is a simple law of energy that says: What you focus on expands; what you believe in will happen. It's a natural outcome of the universal law of attraction, where, due to resonance—or like seeking like—the vibration we put out into the world attracts back to us things of a similar vibration. If you focus on a life story that involves disease, failure, or fear, then that is exactly what you will attract.

The opposite is also true. Take the case of Andrew, a businessman who has investments in many countries, who is living a belief of abundance, gratitude, and sharing. Andrew is always cheerful and excited about his newest venture. He owns companies around the world, including a coffee plantation in Guatemala where all of the plantation's proceeds go back to the village workers.

A New You

Now it's important to assimilate your new beliefs and stories and imprint them into your habits, your thoughts, and all the way to your core. Although, as we've learned, every belief was originally formulated to serve you, beliefs can become outdated and need to evolve. The ideal objective is not to get rid of your old beliefs but to alter them so that they help you achieve your desires and intentions. In the next chapter, we will examine our desires closely to determine which ones are best aligned with our essence and thus most likely to be manifested.

Remember that what you believe is up to you! Use this next exercise to bolster your aspirations.

✧ Claim It! Choose to Believe ✧

In your manifesting journal, write each of the following sentence stems, finishing each with a belief you would like to hold.

- I choose to believe about my potential that . . .

- I choose to believe about my physical body that . . .

- I choose to believe about my social skills that . . .

- I choose to believe about my finances that . . .

- I choose to believe about my future that . . .

- I choose to believe about [fill in your own words] that . . .

I choose!

YOUR DESIRE FORMS THE BASIS OF EVERY MANIFESTATION

Desire is a force from deep inside you, an inherent part of the self. Many times we can be confused between impulses, which are fleeting, and desires, which, when aligned to your essence and your mission, help you manifest the life you envision.

We often get caught wanting more. We are attracted to things we think we need and often convince ourselves that, if we had the next gadget or relationship, our life would be better. No matter how much more you want in your life, it will never be enough if your desires are not connected to your essence. Desire must be clarified, respected, and mined from deep inside you.

When your desires are not aligned to your essence, you will have challenges creating what you want. Your responsibility is to uncover, recognize, and honor your desires. This chapter will help you discover and explore the different aspects of your desires and support you to manifest moment to moment.

Anatomy of Desire

Desire is the most personal of expressions, a composite of the physical, emotional, mental, heart, and spiritual. As we saw in Principle 2, the combination of all of these elements creates an energy and a vibration that is necessary for transformation and moment-to-moment manifestation. To manifest the life you really want, dare to realize what your desires are. Spend time clarifying exactly what it is you want, and realize how it will serve you. Experience each desire as if it has already happened, diving into all the sensations of having attained your dream. In this chapter, we'll show you how to do just that by exploring your desires.

Too often what we think we want is impulsive and doesn't reflect our truth. By exploring your desire in each of the five dimensions, you are more likely to align with your soul longing, which is the basis of manifestation. Let's begin by examining how to experience desire at the physical level.

The Physical Level of Desire

Your body has much to tell you about what you desire. At any time, you have the opportunity to listen to its wisdom. The following exercise, as well as others in this section, is designed to help you connect deeply and truthfully to the desires that lie within you.

❄ Claim It! Body Scan ❄

1. Take a moment and sit in a comfortable position. Close your eyes. Slowly inhale through your nose, imagining that your breath originates in your belly and expands up into your lungs. Hold the breath in for as long as you can, up to a count of 20 (one count per second) and exhale. Repeat this breath at least two more times. Then, allow yourself to breathe normally.

2. From this relaxed place, scan your body. Connect to your feet first, and slowly bring your attention up your legs, into your torso, and into your neck, arms, and head. Witness any sensations, tensions, insights, or teachings that your body is offering.

3. Think of something that you desire to manifest. Feel the energy of that desire within you. You may find that different areas of your body physically experience a heightened level or intensity of sensation. You'll probably be able to identify one area of your body where your desire rests. Keep in mind that there is no "wrong" or "right" answer to feeling this; just trust your instincts and believe you can sense the intensity of the energy.

4. Write about your experience in your manifestation journal.

How does your physical body respond to your desire? Do you experience this sensation in your stomach, your heart, or perhaps your throat? More important, how does it feel: constricted, tight, energized, tense, heavy, or expanded? Tension or constriction in an area of your body may be an indication that your physical body isn't in alignment with your desire. Right now, just witness your experience without making any decisions. When you've finished scanning all five levels of desire, you will have a more complete picture and a clearer understanding of what is standing in the way of your desired manifestations.

The Emotional Level of Desire

Emotion includes within itself the word *motion*. Emotions—both positive and negative—do not have a solid unbending structure. Instead, as we saw in Principle 2, they are flows of energy that constantly change. Too often, we try to "fix" an emotional discomfort in the same way that we would use superglue to repair a broken piece of glass. This might work if the emotion remained solid and unmoving, but in reality, as soon as we identify the discomfort, the emotion has already shifted. This is proven when we "talk something out" with a friend, and the problem becomes easier to handle.

You must simply experience your feelings with compassion and understanding, allowing them to alter, change, evolve, and reconstruct.

⤜ Claim It! Emotional Scan ⤛

1. Take a moment to relax in a quiet place and close your eyes, taking a few deep breaths.

2. Think of the same desire you explored at the physical level of desire.

3. What emotions do you feel when you think of that desire? Peacefulness, joy, excitement, playfulness? How strong is that feeling?

4. Write about your experience in your manifestation journal.

Carefully examine the palette of emotions you access or experience as you consider your desire. Pay special attention to any associations or emotions that could keep you from being able to realize your desire. Express gratitude to the part of yourself that has felt the emotion and allowed you to experience it.

The Mental Level of Desire

The mental level of desire includes your thoughts, perceptions, beliefs, and the internal conversations of your mind. Learning to manage your thoughts and intentions plays a vital role in your moment-to-moment manifestation. (More insights into the relationship between your thinking patterns and what you manifest will continue to be explored in further chapters.)

⚹ Claim It! Mental Scan ⚹

1. Take a moment and sit in a comfortable position. Close your eyes, and take a few deep breaths.

2. Access the same desire you explored at the physical and emotional levels.

3. How do you think about this desire, and how do you talk about it? Listen to yourself. Do you say, "I know it isn't possible, but I would like to . . ." (which limits you because you think it is impossible), or do you say, "I am going to . . ." (which empowers you because it sends a positive command)?

4. How clear and precise are you about what you want? Can you state your desire in its simplest form?

5. Write the simplified statement of your desire in your manifestation journal.

In your mind, visualize a picture of what you desire. Amplify that picture, and add more colors. See yourself in the picture and imagine it in 3-D. Add sounds and feelings to the picture. The more vibrant your mental picture is, the more power you have to manifest. Finally, imagine that this desire has already happened.

The Heart Level of Desire

The heart has its own unique vibration. It brings specific qualities like compassion, love, forgiveness, and gratefulness, which can be experienced most fully through that dimension.

⤙ Claim It! Heart Scan ⤚

1. Sit in a quiet place, close your eyes, and take a few breaths.

2. Access the same desire you explored at the physical, emotional, and mental levels.

3. Connect to your heart. Pay attention to what you experience.

4. Does your heart feel spacious, uplifted? Do you experience tension, pain, or constriction? Does it feel empty or alive? What else do you notice? Does your heart feel vulnerable or strong?

5. Write about your experience in your manifestation journal. At this time, simply witness your experience. As before, there is no need to take action. Acknowledge what you feel on the heart level and move on to explore the spiritual level of desire before assimilating all this information and making a shift in your thoughts and behavior.

Listen to your heart's expression. Its messages are often subtle yet profound.

The Spiritual Level of Desire

The next level is the spiritual dimension; it refers to whatever brings you true meaning and joy in your life—those things that are part of your soul mission.

⤙ Claim It! Spiritual Scan ⤚

1. Find a quiet place, close your eyes, and take a few deep breaths.

2. Access the same desire you explored at the physical, emotional, mental, and heart levels.

3. How will achieving your desire reflect your soul's essence and embody your gifts? How will it serve you and others? Will it support your soul mission and life purpose? Will it expand you and make your heart soar? Will it give you hope, energy, enthusiasm?

4. Take a moment to reflect on what you have discovered about the importance of the spiritual level of desire.

5. Write these realizations in your journal, and allow them to propel you toward manifesting what you truly want.

Now it's time to assess all the information you have received by examining your desire at every level. Each area may offer its own message. Here's how this sequence of exercises worked in Carrol's life.

CARROL'S STORY

For much of my life, I dreamed of owning a red convertible sports car. To me, owning such a car meant claiming my individuality, honoring my creativity, and achieving my soul longing for freedom and playfulness. And yet it was 35 years before I was able to manifest this desire. Let's look at how, by realizing the obstacles on each of the different levels of desire, I was finally able to manifest this particular dream.

Whenever I thought about owning my dream car, I experienced the following:

- **On the physical level:** 1) A sensation of speed, pushing forward from my solar plexus. 2) A tiny sensation of fear at the back of my rib cage. 3) A constriction of my breathing, causing it to be shallow and tentative. Overall, I felt like I was forging ahead with glee and then was pulled back sharply by a leash.

- **On the emotional level:** Excited, joyful, effervescent, thrilled, heavily weighted, resigned. Overall experience: very mixed feelings, much the same as on the physical level.

- **On the mental level:** I see the car and can easily envision myself driving it. I feel the steering wheel under my hands, but then I realize that I'm going nowhere in it. It isn't real.

- **On the heart level:** A feeling of spaciousness and celebration, of gratitude and wonder. Fear is also present.

- **On the spiritual level:** Without doubt, my higher self is worthy of this dream. I see the car as uplifting, inspiring, and nurturing. On the spiritual level, there is no mixed message.

On four out of the five levels of desire, I had established barriers between myself and my desire. Only on the spiritual level was I ready to manifest it. On the other levels, the barriers I had established were holding me back. So, what did I need to do to remedy these incongruities?

Through doing this exercise, I realized why I had not yet manifested my desire. I was sending out mixed messages. On the one hand, I wanted the convertible, but on the other hand, I didn't believe it could happen. I also saw that this behavioral pattern—where I desired something yet held myself back—existed in other areas of my life.

In the case of the red sports car, a common denominator at the physical, mental, and emotional levels was not feeling worthy to realize my desire. I discovered that on the physical, emotional, and mental levels, it felt very uncomfortable to honor myself. For years, I had been a hard worker, committed to winning musical competitions around the world, striving to prove my worth. In addition, I had a tendency to always take care of others before myself. By realizing this and choosing to let go of these old patterns, I began to open up to new possibilities and changed my reality. Simply altering my awareness and attention allowed a shift in what I believed could be real for me.

I now drive a spectacular red convertible and love every minute of it!

Like Carrol, you can examine your desires and see what is needed to clear the way to manifesting them in your life moment to moment. The following exercise will guide you through the process.

⋊ Claim It! Dial a Desire ⋉

1. Take a moment to relax, closing your eyes and taking a few deep breaths.

2. Consider one of your desires. The topic you choose to start with can be anything. Don't stress yourself to find the "perfect desire." What will be uncovered will be of worth to you, no matter what subject you begin with.

3. Ask yourself how you experience that desire in each of the five dimensions:

- Physically

- Emotionally

- Mentally

- In your heart

- Spiritually

4. Are there recurring patterns or commonalities?

5. Do you see these same patterns with other desires or in other areas of your life?

6. How might you alter your awareness and attention pertaining to this desire to better serve you?

You may choose to do this same exercise around a number of different desires in your life. You will probably discover that one or two of the levels of physical, emotional, mental, heart, and spiritual are more vibrant and easier to access than the others. As you examine every layer, notice where you might have any blockages to what you want to manifest. It's fascinating to discover if a parallel pattern appears on several different levels, such as in the physical and emotional, and also in different parts of your life. As you choose to change your relationship with the misalignment in one particular context, you simultaneously impact many other areas of your life.

Ann has always dreamed of owning a house by the water in San Diego. When she explored her desire through the five levels, this is what she discovered: At the physical level, she felt empty, not grounded. At the emotional level, she experienced some anxiety in her chest. At the mental level, she saw a clear picture of her house and the gardens surrounding it. This made her smile! At the heart level, she felt at peace. At the spiritual level, she experienced stillness and saw herself writing books.

Ann was surprised by her discovery that the physical and emotional levels weren't in harmony with her desire but that she was very clear on the other three levels. Looking to see if this lack of physical and emotional alignment was also standing in the way of other things in her life, Ann reflected upon her difficult relationship with her sister. She explored this through the five levels and found the same pattern. At the mental, heart, and spiritual level, Ann was very much in harmony with her desire to be close to her sister. But at the physical level, she felt ungrounded and empty. At the emotional level, there was a lot of turmoil, and Ann realized that her desire was an attachment to an old dream of being close to her sister.

Ann realized how the lack of alignment between the five levels had created so much conflict in her life. She now spends more time listening to her physical and emotional levels, knowing that the insights she receives will help her tremendously to make decisions that will better serve her.

Multi-Level Desire

Now that you have identified your desires and looked at them through the five dimensions of your being, you may have noticed that some levels of your desire aren't aligned. This awareness is an important step to personal transformation, as it will permit you to make the needed adjustments. Without this knowledge, you can get stuck in the following ways:

- If your desire is expressed only at the **physical level**, it becomes a craving; an impulse leading to compulsive behavior.

- If your desire is expressed only at the **emotional level**, it becomes lodged as an attachment and inhibits the flow of energy.

- If your desire is expressed only as a **mental process**, it becomes just a "good idea" that will quickly die.

- If your desire is expressed only at the **heart level**, it will lack boundaries and the reality that is necessary for manifestation to happen.

- If your desire is expressed only at the **spiritual level**, it promotes passive behavior and disconnection while you wait for a miracle to happen (as opposed to *you* being the miracle that makes it happen).

When you take time to connect to a dimension that is not aligned, as Ann did in the previous example, your attention to that misalignment begins a transformational process. This self-examination is beneficial no matter how many times you revisit it.

When your desire is being expressed clearly at every level, that desire is aligned with your inner truth and has a much stronger likelihood of being manifested. The exercise below will support you in being in touch with your true self and help your desires be aligned at the spiritual, heart, mental, emotional, and physical levels.

⋆⟨ Claim It! Morning Blessing ⟩⋆

1. Sit comfortably, preferably in a special place, a safe haven for reflection. There is much to be said for ritual; if you can, establish a sacred place in your home where you can go to rejuvenate.

2. Close your eyes. Take a few deep, slow breaths.

3. Imagine a place you really love. Put yourself there.

4. Connect to one thing about yourself that you are grateful for.

5. Let that thought, that vibration of energy, expand like a wave of light, to every cell of your being. Stay in this space as long as you wish. Allow this feeling, like a halo, to surround, energize, and protect you throughout the whole day.

Each day, as you finish this exercise, take out your journal and write down what about yourself fills you with joy and what you are grateful for. Make this statement in the present tense. Allow it to serve as your personal mantra, your vitamin C for the soul. You have taken another important step toward manifesting your essence. In the next chapter, we'll look at the crucial role of a clear and focused intention.

Intention Overcomes Every Obstacle

You've done a lot of the core work that is essential to affecting your potential to manifest. From uncovering your soul mission to aligning the five dimensions of your desire, you have built for yourself a firm foundation for manifestation.

The next step in the manifestation process is to establish a clear and focused intention, or intent. Your intention brings energy and focus and is a vital part of being able to manifest what you want. In this chapter, you'll learn how to develop the power and quality of your intention. You will also look at some of the blocks that may happen when you're trying to stay committed to your intention.

There are three main components that will help you create a powerful intent: your desire, your thoughts and the ability to stay focused on them, and the clarity of what you want. In the previous chapter, you explored the quality of your desires. We suggest that for every intention you create, you scan your corresponding desire, using the five dimensions to understand where possible obstacles may occur. Now we will examine the importance of intentional thought.

The Power of Thought

Your thoughts are your inner reality, your potential, and your realm of possibility. Thoughts can be constructive or destructive for your life. Writers and philosophers have been aware of the power of thought throughout history. Buddha said, "You are what you think." According to Sikh spiritual leader Yogi Bhajan, "There is nothing more powerful than thought. Everything starts from thought." Claude M. Bristol, one of the first foundational coaches, was visionary in his 1948 book, *The Magic of Believing*. He wrote: "Thought is the original source of all wealth, all success, all material gain, all great discoveries and inventions, and of all achievements." Ralph Waldo Emerson, American writer, lecturer, and poet of the 19th century wrote: "The ancestor of every action is thought."

Sometimes we are aware of the thoughts that drive our actions, and sometimes we are not. Very often we career through life, reacting to the thoughts that we think are ours but may stem from other voices from the past, from preconceived ideas or reactions to experiences, from our efforts to be the "person you should be," or from myriad other irrelevant sources. Instead of creating your reality in this way, become aware of your thoughts and intentions, and clear the way to manifestation.

What You Think So You Will Become

The law of attraction is based on the concept that like attracts like. What you think about will be attracted to you, and the energy a person exudes will attract a similar energy. If you are very positive, you will energetically attract positive outcomes.

Esther and Jerry Hicks, in their books and seminars on the law of attraction, have offered transformational insights into the power that your thoughts have upon your reality. In their words, "Every thought vibrates, every thought radiates a signal, and every thought attracts a matching signal back."[1]

We have all met people who have chronic health problems. They constantly talk about their ill health and the associated difficulties. By their attention to it, they're attracting further bad health. One way to help themselves turn the situation around is to begin to focus on the positive aspects of their lives and think constantly about how much better they feel each day and how they are healing.

It is often easier to express what you don't want rather than what you do want. For example, consider the thought *I don't want to work this weekend.* Because this thought pattern includes the suggestion of work, working is most likely what the person will do, even though that is not their desire. According to Neuro-Linguistic Programming, the brain doesn't understand the word *don't.* It just processes the concept of *work this weekend.* To be more successful in your mental and verbal commands, say what you want to do this weekend: "I want to relax this weekend," "I want to really unwind and get outside in my garden," and so on.

Learn to think *only what you want, not what you don't want!* This sounds simple but in fact requires constant attention. As you set your intent, make sure to focus on the positive outcomes you want to manifest.

Setting Your Intent

Setting your intent is not to be confused with goal setting. Goal setting focuses on attaining a specific outcome, whereas setting your intent involves examining and attracting what will serve your soul mission.

As you set your intent, be as open and positive as possible. Approach it from a creative vantage point using your right brain, the associative and intuitive brain, to give birth to your intent. Take your time with this process. If you go too quickly, there is a tendency to be linear, and you may create unnecessary pressure, which will limit your possibilities.

Allow yourself to be free and creative. Toward attaining that, we've provided four different activities in the following Claim It! sections that will be helpful as you clarify and focus your intentions.

⚡ Claim It! Create It! ⚡

The first activity to express and clarify your intention is to make a manifestation board.

1. Get a poster-sized sheet, scissors, and glue.

2. Gather a stack of magazines and calendars and/or pictures you've taken.

3. Select and cut out pictures you are attracted to that connect to your intent.

4. Glue these images to your paper or poster board in a way that pleases you. There is no logic to how you do this; no plan, no strategy.

5. Put this collage in a place where you will be reminded of your intent every day (on your desktop, the wall of your office, and so on).

⤜ Claim It! See It! ⤛

The second activity is to do a daily visualization.

1. Close your eyes and sit in a comfortable position.

2. Take a couple of deep, relaxing breaths.

3. If you choose, put on some soft music in the background.

4. Visualize yourself having attained your intent. Focus on different aspects of this scene, making it as real as possible. What time of day is it? Where are you? Who else is in your picture? How do you feel? Stay with this picture for five minutes.

5. Repeat this process every day, as your intentional focus on it draws it more and more into your reality.

⤜ Claim It! Write It! ⤛

The third activity is to write in your manifestation journal every day.

1. Start your journaling by saying, "I am so grateful that [whatever you intend] has happened." By anticipating that you have already attained what you want, you magnify the process.

2. After your gratitude, write freely about your feelings surrounding your intent.

✦ Claim It! Stick to It! ✦

The fourth activity is to remind yourself constantly of your intent.

1. Write your intent on sticky notes and put them everywhere: in your house, your office, your car, and so forth.

2. Establish an association between your intent and a piece of jewelry, clothing, or a crystal. Every time you see this item, you will be reminded of the importance of your intent.

Remember, the more you focus on what you want, the greater the likelihood that you will manifest it. A number of factors can interfere with our ability to sustain an intense concentration on our intent, and it's important to understand them so we can make sure they don't interfere with our ability to manifest.

When You Disconnect from Your Intent

There are many ways we can get disconnected from our essence and our intentions.

We can get extremely busy doing things that we don't really love but think are necessary. We might be hooked into a business that is financially rewarding but not fulfilling, or we may be in a relationship that isn't nurturing. When this happens, it is easy to disconnect from our true self and dismiss the importance of our desires and intentions.

Let's explore some situations that can create a disconnect between you and your intention and cause you to freeze, not knowing what to do next or how to handle the situation.

Many people become frozen with indecision as they try to figure out what is exactly the next "right" move, or what will help them the most. Often that anxiety comes from trying to figure out the "how to" and losing track of the intention.

Getting stuck in the "how" can especially be a problem for those in the corporate world. Often precious resources and time are spent on figuring out exactly the right next move, the "how." Instead of remaining trapped in this restricted view, focus on the vision and the motivation that fuel the excitement to discover and achieve. Don't get stuck in the "how." Instead, say *yes* to movement and innovation. Move! Try something new. Motion, *any* motion, is a positive step. As Yogi Bhajan said, "When the pressure is on you, *start*, and the pressure will be off."[2]

Another situation you may face is expecting a perfect moment to set your intent. Perfection is a fallacy. Do not fall into the trap of waiting until everything is exactly the way it should be. When you are ready, it's too late. Now is always the perfect time to take action.

Another way people often get stuck is in the "spin." This feels like being in a whirling dervish of trapped energy. You feel uncertain about how to proceed and fraught with indecision. The longer you are uncertain and anxious about what action to take, the more immobile you become, and the deeper into the "spin" you go. Unfortunately the deeper into the "spin" you get, the more everything seems hopeless and the more you feel trapped. It seems like the situation is taking over. You are overwhelmed and cannot think, cannot function. You are spinning!

Again, the solution is action! At this point, any action is a success. Taking a step, any step, will cause a different chain of events and, much like turning the kaleidoscope from the exercise in Principle 4, will offer new opportunities for clarity of mind and positive decisions. Here's how Carrol experienced it:

CARROL'S STORY

I was having the worst time trying to clear the clutter of papers on my desk, though I really wanted it to be done. I would pick up a piece of paper and then put it down because I was indecisive about what to do with it. I would pick up another piece of paper, maybe a bill, and remember that I needed to call the company to check if it was accurate or not. But that involved finding some other papers (Agh!) so I put that paper back down.

I was in a spin. Every time I was unable to complete a necessary step, I slid further down into the vortex of unfulfilled energy. Accompanying this terrifying dive was self-recrimination ("I should have done that weeks ago!"), emotional fatigue, and finally paralysis.

Remembering that the antidote for the spin is action, I decided to choose just one piece of paper and take action on it. At the bottom of the pile, I found a phone number related to a (by now outdated) request for a musician, and I telephoned the agency. I was surprised when the woman I spoke with offered me a new opportunity to perform, and for much more money! Not only did a nice new opportunity arise, but I was also astounded at how little time this simple action took. Refreshed and enthused, I was confident to take more steps and not be trapped in the energy tornado I had experienced so often. As the "spin" energy cleared, a variety of new possibilities opened up.

You can experience the same release of energy, using the same process. This next exercise will help.

> ## ·⌇ Claim It! It's All About Action ⌇·
>
> 1. Imagine a situation that is anxiety ridden and causes you to spin. The situation may be clearing your desk, preparing your income taxes, or making a difficult phone call. It might be deciding about a move or job change or about interactions with a difficult family member.
>
> 2. Pretend you know what to do.
>
> 3. Take action, any action. Immediately, your action will cause a different outcome, a new scenario, and a wealth of new options that are free of association and accompanying stress. You will be unstuck.

Use this exercise to explore other areas of your life where you experience the spin.

While we've seen how distraction can pull us away from focusing on our intent, it is also important to consider the source of our motivation. The success of manifestation is impacted by whether our motivation is based in passion or pressure.

Your Motivation: Passion or Pressure?

When your motivation comes from your true self, it's easier to stay focused on your intent. When your motivation comes from fear, getting frozen is predictable and setting or following through on your intentions becomes more difficult.

Passion motivation is generated by excitement and the enthusiasm to create what uplifts you. It comes from inside and serves your soul. It focuses on what you truly want. This motivation is particularly easy to express in positive thought patterns, such as, "I really love running, and I want to do the next marathon."

Because this motivation is from a source deep within you, it will be minimally affected by external circumstances.

On the other hand, pressure motivation focuses on fear and what you don't want to create. It's a motivation generated by adrenaline. An example from the business world is, "If we don't improve our sales, we'll need to lay off employees." This is short-term, fear-based motivation, dependent upon outside events. It is a survival mechanism that can never be as fulfilling as being motivated by inspiration, creativity, and passion.

The following exercise is designed to help you recognize where you are motivated by either passion or pressure.

❋ Claim It! Who Is Running Your Life? ❋

1. Write down 5 to 10 topics, each one representing a part of your life, an activity, or an ongoing desire. Your list could include what you do, what you love, what inspires you or stresses you, and so on.

2. Look at your list and consider your motivation behind each item. For every topic, assess the following on a scale of 1 to 10 (1 = *not at all,* 10 = *completely*):

- Is this Passion based?

- Is this Fear or Pressure based?

3. Revisit each item on your list that was primarily motivated by pressure. What can you learn about that pressure? Ask yourself:

- *Why did I first get attracted to this?*

- *What parts of it do I feel passionate about?*

> • *How can I tweak my relationship with this to focus on the parts that I feel passionate about and that bring me joy?*
>
> • *What can I change today that will positively affect my life?*

TEJPAL'S STORY

I decided to take the challenge of this exercise. Here's my list:

My yard:

- Passion = 8: I can visualize a peaceful yard without weeds and clutter. This gives me a sense of serenity.

- Pressure = 6: I always seem to put work on the top of my priorities and never take the time to address this situation. That causes pressure.

My work:

- Passion = 8: My work uplifts me. It's aligned with my soul mission, which is to help men and women discover and redesign their life around their purpose.

- Pressure = 3: I sometimes overcommit and work too many hours per week.

Physical activity:

- Passion = 9: Being challenged at the physical level is playful and fun for me. It energizes me and clears my mind. It gives me a positive spirit.

- Pressure = 1: At times, I push myself too hard, and it stops being fun.

Creative arts:

- Passion = 10: Whether it's pottery, painting, playing the guitar, singing, or cooking, I experience flow and fun when I do these artistic activities.

- Pressure = 2: When something is new, like throwing clay on a wheel, I sometimes struggle, get impatient, and tense up.

Tejpal's use of this exercise suggests that her life is reflecting the passion-based intents that are in tune with her soul mission. The exercise can also be used to check your current activities against your soul mission and move your life in a new direction, as Peter did.

Peter, who is a client, created this list, using our exercise to reflect on the direction of his life's work.

1. I work at a middle school and have been there ten years.

- Passion: 0
- Pressure: 9
- Reflection: I need to keep my job to support my family, but it's not personally rewarding. I am so bored! I feel trapped, and I'm exhausted.

2. I like to help at the children's hospital.

- Passion: 9
- Pressure: 1
- Reflection: I love the spirit there. These children love to play and are so grateful for my presence! We play games. Maybe I need to get a paying job

there or look at job situations where my creative abilities are welcomed.

3. Health

- Passion: 2
- Pressure: 8
- Reflection: I have to lose weight. My doctor told me that the extra pounds I'm carrying are harming my heart.

4. Art and creative projects

- Passion: 10
- Pressure: 0
- Reflection: I love helping my children build their log cabin. It allows my creativity to flourish.

As Peter reviewed the questions in step 3 of the Claim It! and examined his list, he was struck by the importance of creativity in his life. He knew he was first attracted to teaching at a public school because he felt so strongly about having an impact on children. When he asked himself if he still felt passionate about any parts of his job—listed as pressure motivated in the exercise—he thought about the opportunity to be a positive influence and ignite in his students the passion to learn. He realized that he would really enjoy getting his students to do creative projects that taught them scientific principles, such as making a wind machine, creating a garden, and making a solar-powered oven.

He decided to call a friend who was very creative and asked that friend to stop by his classroom the next day so they could discuss these ideas further. The pressure he felt going to work began to change to passion as he changed what he would do with the students.

Motivation Shift

If you find that much of your life is driven by pressure and not passion, it will be more challenging for you to manifest what you want because you have limited opportunity to connect to your true essence and your desire. But you have the power to shift this paradigm. Peter's example shows that you *are* capable of altering the quality of your motivation. When you realize that you're being more motivated by pressure than by passion, here is a simple exercise that is available to you at all times.

⚒ Claim It! On the Other Hand ⚒

1. Put your two hands out, palms up.

2. In your left hand, imagine something that has been a worry to you. For example, "On the one hand, I always feel pressure about paying my mortgage."

3. Then look at the other hand and shift the problem to see it in a different way. You could say, "But on the other hand, I have a lot of equity in that house, and it's a great security to me. And I love it. It also offers me stability and a sense of belonging."

4. Repeat steps 2 and 3 several times to see multiple facets of the same situation.

Notice how, as you recognize the pressures and passion associated with the situation, your cognizance of the challenge changes. By altering your perspective to realize the possibilities of what might be and appreciating the situation from a different vantage point, you're able to change from experiencing pressure to experiencing your passion.

Another way to shift your motivation and stay focused on your intention is to work on your breath. As we have mentioned several times throughout this book, your breath is a powerful tool to help you shift.

⚔ Claim It! Reboot Your System ⚔

1. Sit in a comfortable position. Block your right nostril with the right index finger for this whole exercise.

2. Inhale in four strokes through the left nostril. Hold the breath in for a count of five.

3. Exhale in four strokes (through the left nostril only). Hold the breath out for the same count.

4. As you are able, expand the length of time that you hold the breath in and out.

5. Repeat this cycle for a minimum of three minutes.

You've learned in this chapter to stay focused on your intention to create your desired manifestation. Remember that your thoughts and your intentions can overcome any obstacle.

The Power to Choose

Viktor Frankl, an Austrian Jew who survived the atrocities of the Holocaust in a concentration camp, has written numerous books inspiring millions of people. He offers this confirmation of the freedom to choose our thoughts and intentions:

". . . everything can be taken from a man but one thing: the last of human freedoms—to choose one's attitude in any given set of circumstances, to choose one's own way."[3]

We all have the freedom and ability to change our attitude and our thoughts, and to live our lives with intention and passion on a moment-to-moment basis. In the next chapter, you will keep developing your self-awareness about who you are and what you really want. From the vantage point of the chakra system, you will explore different aspects of your life and discover for yourself what is serving you and what needs altering so you can move quickly toward realizing your dreams.

You Have the Power to Clear, Heal, and Reinvent Constantly

Thus far in this book we've examined many different ways to enhance your ability to manifest. Each chapter has helped you to clear away blocks holding you back and strengthen your ability to access your unique essence. Like a miner, you have dug deep inside yourself to uncover your soul mission and your authentic desires. You have examined your stories and beliefs and realized their influence on your life, and you've learned how to change those that are no longer serving you to manifest what you want. You have empowered your intuition and set your intent. And you've discovered the power of energy, a tool so important for manifesting that we will explore it further in this chapter.

As you learned in Principle 2, you and everything around you is made up of energy. This is substantiated in many teachings, from ancient spiritual traditions to quantum physics. Each of us has our own personal energy field—called the human energy field. As you align and strengthen your energy field, you facilitate manifesting the life you truly desire. You do this by working with a key dimension of the human energy field, the chakra system.

The Power of the Chakra System

Chakra is a Sanskrit word that means "wheel of light." There are seven main chakras found throughout the body that affect your physical, emotional, and spiritual balance. Imagine these chakras as wheels of light located at different points in your body, each one a vortex of energy. Each chakra has a specific purpose and vibration that can serve as a basis for clearing and reenergizing elements of your life that may be standing in your way to manifesting what you desire.

Throughout this chapter, we'll first help you strengthen each chakra and then examine the aspect of your life that the chakra corresponds to.

©iStock Photo - Shannon Kegan; adapted by Christie McMearty

The Chakra System

The First Chakra: Clearing Your Space

The first chakra is often called the root chakra and is located at the base of your spine. This chakra represents your foundation. When it's in balance, you feel present, centered, grounded, and ready to take action. When it's out of balance, you feel overwhelmed and paralyzed.

On the physical level, the first chakra affects the organs of elimination. On the emotional and spiritual levels, it corresponds to clearing and letting go. On the mental level, this chakra impacts clarity of thought and the ability to simplify, focus, and eliminate.

Your surroundings are a reflection of your energy field. If your personal environment is cluttered and stagnant, this indicates an imbalance in the first chakra. Clearing your physical space will create vibrational clarity in your energy field that you can feel in your whole body. This greatly influences your ability to think clearly, be creative, and manifest. You can also use the first chakra as a vehicle to clear your physical environment. Begin by energizing the first chakra with the following exercise.

⊰ Claim It! Clear and Energize Your First Chakra ⊱

1. Stand with your feet shoulder-width apart and shoulders relaxed.

2. Inhale quickly, imagining you are inhaling the color red (the color of the first chakra).

3. Then squat down on your heels, exhaling slowly and saying, "Haaaa."

4. Do this seven times. Each time you exhale, be aware of how you are releasing tension and stress.

5. This cycle may be repeated three times for maximum benefit.

Notice that with this chakra energized you feel a relaxed energy that allows you more clarity and the ability to take action without questioning yourself. You are grounded.

Now that you have strengthened your first chakra, take a look at your surroundings. See if there is clutter or clarity, if you feel confusion or serenity. Don't underestimate the power of clutter. There is a common misconception that small annoyances aren't important. But, in fact, you will be shocked by how much weight is immediately lifted off your shoulders when that seemingly small stress is removed. Something like a broken object may seem inconsequential, but actually carries with it an energy that affects you every time you view it or even think of it. In addition, you may have negative associations with an object, even though on some level you like it. For example, a picture taken at a time when you were unhappy will remind you of those negative feelings every time you look at it.

TEJPAL'S STORY

Many years ago, I was renting an office space in Connecticut. I was traveling quite a bit then and would be away from my office for days or even weeks at a time. Every time I returned to my office, I immediately focused on a large stain in the middle of my carpet. It always annoyed me, but I would rationalize that the stain was okay.

One day I decided to hire an organizational coach to help me implement a more effective business system and a feng shui expert to complement the work by creating beauty and efficiency at the energetic level. It became immediately apparent from both vantage points that it was time to take action and have the stain removed. When I finally did this, the relief I felt was amazing! Suddenly I could relax and be present in my work space without that nagging discomfort in the back of my mind.

Perhaps you've "looked" but not "seen" your environment with true awareness. Does your space serve you? What elements are not necessary or helpful to you at this time in your life but are still a part of your story because they remain in your space? Now it's time for you to do the physical clearing: throw away, eliminate, clear, and rejuvenate. As you clear your space you will simultaneously clear and rejuvenate yourself on the mental and emotional levels. The following exercise will walk you through this process.

⚜ Claim It! Clear It! ⚜

1. Choose a room in your home or work environment.

2. Look at each item in that space and ask the following three questions:

- *Do I need this?*

- *Have I used it in the last six months?*

- *Are all of my emotional associations with it positive?*

3. Evaluate your answers to these questions and decide if that item is necessary or beneficial to you.

4. If not, clear it out. Even one negative answer to the previous questions is grounds for eliminating the item from your space.

Kristen was a journalist who decided to clear out the office space in her home. When she began the process, it seemed an overwhelming and impossible task. She had accumulated papers, journals, receipts, unanswered mail, and assorted office supplies for years. When she did the exercise, she was astounded at the amount of paperwork she didn't need that simply added to her clutter. She was also fascinated to learn that although many of her office supplies were used and useful, they had negative emotional anchors that reminded her of a difficult project that had recently been concluded. These emotions were so strong that the mere use of the office supplies rendered her incapable of forward motion.

Each item she cleared made the job easier. After the clearing was complete, she not only had a more serene working environment, but also got to buy new office supplies, which carried with them the energy of rejuvenation. Kristen is now far more productive in that environment and achieves more than she ever thought possible.

The Second Chakra: Clearing Time and Creating Flow

The second chakra is located below your navel and is associated with your reproductive system. It represents creativity, intimacy, playfulness, pleasure, and spontaneity. When this chakra is in balance, you are able to listen to your intuition and express yourself freely. When it's out of balance, you second-guess yourself, constrict your creativity, and are unable to see the big picture. This can cause you to struggle with time management. The second chakra relates to physical and sexual vitality. On the emotional and spiritual levels, this chakra affects your ability to trust and honor your feelings. On the mental level, it involves being secure enough to entertain new ideas.

When the second chakra is out of balance, we experience a constriction, tightness, and a lack of spontaneity. These conditions impact how a person is able to manage his or her time. Some people may experience a need to structure, plan, and organize to a fault. Excessive time management is very linear and doesn't allow enough space to empower the creative process. Other people may experience the opposite response to their second chakra being out of balance, becoming lackadaisical, maybe unable to pay bills on time or complete projects.

By strengthening the second chakra, and examining your relationship with time, you will experience greater creativity and ease in many areas of your life. This balancing facilitates the natural flow of manifestation. A simple way to balance this chakra is with the following, a Kundalini yoga posture called "Sufi Grind."[1]

❊ Claim It! Clear and Energize the Second Chakra ❊

1. Sit on the floor with your legs crossed.

2. Put your hands on your knees.

3. Move the spine in a big circle in one direction for one minute, and then the opposite direction for the same amount of time. Your head will stay relatively level, and your chest and heart center will remain open.

4. At the end, take a deep breath, imagining the color orange flowing through your body (the color of the second chakra), and relax.

Now that you've strengthened your second chakra, let's explore how the power of this chakra can assist you in your relationship with time.

Time Out

When we feel rushed or believe there isn't enough time, we often feel anxiety.

Instead of thinking that there is a deficiency of time in life, experience time as a component of abundance. When we concentrate on time limitations, we restrict the creative flow that will allow for the discovery of solutions with ease and spontaneity. We usually view time as a linear element that passes by, constantly moving forward. However, if we choose to see time as a nonlinear element, we open up to new possibilities.

The answer is not the actual amount of time available, but rather the way you view and use it. For example, the more time you allow for a project, the more time it needs. Tejpal has trained many leaders to produce more in less time, encouraging them to "keep it simple" and to call on their creativity and innovation. One of them was Andrea.

Andrea held an important position in the human-resources department of a multinational company. Every night she would work until at least 8 P.M., finishing up projects and preparing for the following day. Then she discovered a passion for salsa dancing and joined a dance class that met twice a week at 6 P.M. She was surprised to realize that on the two days a week of her dance class, she finished all the work she needed to in much less time and was able to go dancing.

When Andrea discovered her real passion and joy in life, she also found the time to pursue it. When her priorities shifted, she realized that she could be more effective with less time and was able to explore her creativity. We suggest that you look at different areas of your life to assess how you spend your time so that it supports the life you want to manifest.

⚜ Claim It! Quite a Slice ⚜

Let's examine your relationship with time and your ability to balance all the elements of your life.

1. On a piece of paper, draw a circle. This is the "pie" of your life. Draw in pieces of the pie, with each piece representing an element of your life.

2. Label each piece. Perhaps you will have pieces for "family," "job," "self-care," and so on.

3. Now consider each piece of the pie separately as you exercise awareness and integration. Ask yourself four questions:

- *How do I feel when I think of this part of my life? How much time do I allow for it? Do I want to reconsider this time commitment?*

- *How would I like this area to feel?*

- *What is the one thing that I can change today to create more flow in this area of my life?*

- *How will I know when I have successfully made the change?*

4. To clear your relationship with time, work with one area until it feels spacious and balanced. Concentrate on one area at a time. Don't be concerned at this point with the other slices you aren't pursuing. There will be "time" for those later. When you stay in the moment without worrying about the next step, you allow the manifestation process to work at its best.

The Third Chakra: Clearing Self-Judgment

The third chakra is located at the solar plexus, between the navel and the bottom of the sternum. This energy vortex has to do with ego, will, strength, and the spiritual warrior within. When it is balanced, you feel confident and at peace with who you are. You are comfortable enough to express your authentic self. When it is unbalanced, you experience self-judgment and doubts, and you expend energy trying to be somebody you're not. You get stuck worrying about who you "should be" instead of experiencing who you truly are.

On the physical level, the third chakra affects the organs of the digestive system. On the emotional and spiritual levels, it corresponds to self-love and self-nurturing. On the mental level, this chakra impacts your ability to stay neutral and be able to discern instead of judge.

Let's begin by strengthening your third chakra.

❊ Claim It! Clear and Energize Your Third Chakra ❊

1. In a seated position, place your hands on your knees.

2. Inhale through the nose and flex the spine, bringing your torso forward.

3. Then exhale through the nose as you flex your spine toward the back. Keep your head level as you do this exercise.[2]

4. Continue for one to three minutes.

5. Relax and inhale deeply through your nose as you visualize the color yellow (the color of the third chakra). Hold the breath in and visualize that color expanding in your body for a few seconds and then exhale forcefully through the mouth.

6. Repeat this breathing process three times. Feel the renewed energy flowing through your third chakra.

Self-judgment is often held in the third chakra. It can be a huge block to creating any desired manifestation. It causes you to focus on your limitations and on what appears to be impossible. From such a position you shut down and experience anger and anxiety. Your mind then takes over, creating stories and excuses, and actually manifests roadblocks, which causes you to disconnect from your essence. Focusing on your limitations can also be the root of creating self-destructive behaviors, including too much alcohol, food, caffeine, or even too much work and no time to balance and rejuvenate.

A simple way to unplug the mind from this self-sabotaging is to claim the discomfort. Take an honest look at what you perceive as your personal limitations. The moment you bring your hidden weaknesses to light and name your fears, you have taken a powerful step toward overcoming their influence on you. In the following exercise, you can give a voice to your internal thought process, especially to the judgmental part of yourself.

⚔ Claim It! "Be Yourself; Everyone Else Is Taken"[3] ⚖

1. Think of all the aspects of yourself that you don't like and write them down. These elements could be physical, mental, emotional, or spiritual in nature.

2. As you write your list, accept that what you don't like doesn't have to make logical sense.

3. Every judgment has an emotion connected to it, and you may be surprised by the strength of some of the feelings you uncover. Understand that connecting to the part of you that you don't like, with an open heart, will not sabotage or hurt you. In fact, the opposite is true. As you accept and integrate these feelings, you are diminishing the power they have to limit you and thus setting yourself free of them.

4. Thank yourself for feeling strong enough to let these inner voices make themselves known. Return to this exercise a number of times to develop more clarity.

By recognizing and listing the self-judgments you've been holding, you deepen your compassion and sensitivity to yourself and others. As you accept your vulnerability, you open up to the possibility for change, healing, and manifestation on a very deep level.

Now that you've connected with your self-judgments, let's explore how you can challenge those judgments and alter your perception. The process of challenging any given statement, a technique based on Neuro-Linguistic Programming, can have a strong impact on altering our beliefs and the way we see ourselves. Whatever you say or think that you hear as self-judgment, such as "I can't do that," can be challenged with phrases such as, "Am I sure I can't?" "How do I know that is true?" "How has this been proven to be real and not just my interpretation?" "What would it look like and feel like, if this were not true?"

There are many questions that can "unstick" a limiting belief. Further, you don't need to wait to do this until a thought pattern becomes ingrained. Try to catch limiting thoughts the second they occur. For example, if you feel a sore throat coming on, you might think, *I always get sick.* Counter that with, *Well, not always. I haven't had a cold for months. I think this is just momentary . . .*

❊ Claim It! Challenge That Self-Judgment ❊

- Look again at the list you made in your journal of all the aspects of yourself that you don't like.

- Challenge yourself on every limiting statement that you hold about yourself.

- For every item, be as creative as possible in challenging that statement. Ask yourself, *Is that true? How do I know that really happened?* and similar questions as listed in the previous paragraphs. See it in its truest essence, rather than experiencing it as being overwhelming and powerful.

This process doesn't need to be complicated; in fact, it is stronger if kept simple. By accessing and working with what you have considered your least ideal traits and habits, you've taken important action in overcoming their negative impact on your success and your potential to manifest.

The Fourth Chakra: Clearing Relationships

The fourth chakra is often called the heart center and is located at the center of the chest. This chakra helps you create harmony between your mind, body, and spirit. When it is in balance, you are able to love everything: people, plants, animals, and yourself. You understand through compassion. When it is out of balance, you experience fear, lack of trust, and disconnection with yourself and everything around you.

On the physical level, the fourth chakra affects the heart and the lungs. On the emotional and spiritual levels, it corresponds to connectedness, forgiveness, and gratitude. On the mental level, this chakra helps you stay open and welcoming to everything, even what you don't understand. Now let's strengthen our fourth chakra using an ancient Hawaiian technique called Ho'oponopono.

This technique has a fascinating history that will help you appreciate its power. Dr. Stanley Hew Len, a clinical psychologist and the leading expert in Ho'oponopono, was employed by the Hawaii State Hospital Clinic for the Criminally Insane. Dr. Hew Len had extraordinary results healing the mentally ill patients institutionalized there, and he did so without working directly on them. He would study the file of each patient, and then he would access that problem within his own body. He would then think of the patient and repeat the phrase, "I Love You, I'm Sorry, Please Forgive Me, Thank You." Over the course of Dr. Hew Len's work, every patient in the facility was taken off sedatives and removed from solitary confinement or restraints. The impact of his work was so strong that eventually every person was healed, and the hospital was closed.[4]

You can use Dr. Hew Len's technique in your own life, as follows.

Claim It! Clear and Energize Your Fourth Chakra

1. Bring to your mind something that distresses you or brings you physical or mental discomfort. Hold that thought in your mind.

2. Repeat to yourself, "I love you. I'm sorry. Please forgive me. Thank you." You can repeat this as many times as you need, and repeat it at different times in your day.

3. Allow the problem to be healed, released, and cleared.

4. You don't need to understand exactly how this works; simply trust the healing power of the heart.

Everything in life is based on relationships. Whether you are buying or selling something, asking for help or giving support, the quality of your relationships, personal and professional, affect your ability to create what you want. Nothing about manifestation is done alone. We always have people on our path to challenge or support us in anything we accomplish or attract. The power of the heart is vital to the success of your relationships. In the next exercise, we invite you to heal relationships that may be preventing you from manifesting the life you truly desire.

⚔ Claim It! Healing Relationships ⚔

Choose a relationship in your life that is uncomfortable for you and causes you distress.

Close your eyes and detect where that is lodged in your physical body. You may just intuitively know it is there. For example, if you are visual you may see a place where there is some darkness; if you are kinesthetic, you may feel a tension somewhere in your body such as your stomach, your shoulders, behind your eye, and so on. Simply locate where it is.

You have the power to heal this distressful relationship by utilizing the wisdom of the physical body. Follow these steps:

1. *Align:* Prepare yourself to be centered and in the moment. Ground yourself by taking a few deep breaths.

2. *Set Your Intent:* Our intents are often unclear and hold mixed messages. Realize that the more positive and clear your intentions are, the more powerful and effective your healing will be. Begin by asking what your true intention is. Do you really want to heal this relationship? Be honest with yourself. On a scale from 1 to 10, where are you with your desire to heal this situation? This seems like a simple question, but one of the most important elements of healing or manifesting whatever you desire is to have a clear intent. Imagine what the relationship will be like when cleared and healed.

3. *Believe:* At this very moment, do you believe you can heal this relationship? As you've learned earlier in this book, your belief is a powerful force in any transformation you want to create.

4. *Connect:* Connect at the physical level to your place of pain. Every emotional pain that we feel has a corresponding location in the physical body. Try to locate where that is. You may choose to put your hand on that place. Experience all the information that place is offering you. Sense and embrace what is offered. You don't need to *do* anything to the pain; just receive it, hold the space, and it will transform.

5. *Allow:* As you stay connected to your place of pain, open up to any images that come to you. You may see an animal, a flower, or another part of nature. It may be a color or just a feeling. Just receive this, don't judge. When you judge, you disconnect. Remain open for three to four minutes to whatever this experience offers you.

6. *Close:* Take a deep breath and relax as you complete your healing work. Seal your experience with gratitude and appreciation.

The Fifth Chakra: Truth and Finances

The fifth chakra is located at the throat. It represents your social identity and the ability to speak your truth and express your own needs. When the fifth chakra is in balance, you'll experience a consistency between your actions and your words. You are not afraid to say what you need, and you feel a sense of self-esteem. When it is out of balance, you may experience an inability to honor yourself.

On the physical level, the fifth chakra affects the thyroid and parathyroid glands. On the emotional and spiritual levels, it corresponds to claiming your birthright and attracting what you want. On the mental level, this chakra impacts the ability to set boundaries and to be able to realize what you need and deserve.

An imbalance in your fifth chakra is often reflected in, though not limited to, a disharmony in your financial affairs. Money represents a blueprint for how you operate in life: how you set your boundaries to yourself and others, how you value what your needs are, and how you follow through with your commitments. When you come into alignment with your finances, great clarity will be gained in many aspects of your life. Finances represent an outward expression of your inner reality. The following exercise will assist you in energetically clearing and strengthening your fifth chakra.

⚜ Claim It! Clear and Energize Your Fifth Chakra ⚜

1. In a seated position, close your eyes and relax. Begin to roll your neck slowly in one direction for about 30 seconds and then switch directions.

2. Next, take a deep breath in, imagining your body being encompassed with sky blue (the color of the fifth chakra).

3. As you slowly exhale, chant the sound "Oh," clearing all the air from your lungs.

4. Repeat this four more times.

5. Now repeat the same process, chanting "Eeee" and then, "Aahhh."

We live in a world of financial seduction. Credit cards and loans can pull us out of experiencing "what really is" and cause us, when we abuse them, to lose our integrity. It is even possible to buy something without paying for many months. Somewhere inside you, however, this causes a disconnect because your spirit knows the situation isn't logical. This serves as an invitation to become ungrounded and to fall out of alignment with yourself.

Your relationship with your finances is a mirror of your internal reality. When it is out of balance, you may spend all your time thinking about the future, dreaming about endless possibilities and an unrealistic cash flow. You create an endless wish list in your mind, and use your credit cards to the max. Or, to the contrary, you may be afraid to take risks or open up to any new possibilities. You might spend too much time controlling and managing your expenses instead of focusing on opportunities for more abundance. Another possibility is to be anchored in the past, having difficulty letting go of things that don't serve you anymore and carrying too many debts. Clearing your relationship with money will open up many new possibilities, allowing you to reinvent yourself and to manifest what you desire.

What we invite you to focus on is not your current financial state, but the much more important question: What is your relationship with money? On the one hand, you may feel empowered and full of enthusiasm when you think of your financial situation. You can envision all that might be possible based on your experience and financial reality. On the other hand, you may experience a sense of panic, dread, or stress. Let's explore it through the following exercise:

⋅⟨ Claim It! Flashlight of the Soul ⟩⋅

1. Pretend you have an imaginary flashlight. Just like any flashlight, its purpose is to shed light on whatever you point it at. In this case, shine your flashlight on all the different aspects of your relationship with money.

2. When you shine the flashlight and look at your finances, what do you experience? How do you feel? Are you immobilized and afraid to dig too deep because of what you might discover? Rather than focusing on your situation, become aware of your state of being and inner experience as you examine your finances. By becoming aware of and assessing your reactions and habits, you can create a fundamental shift in how you clear the stress you feel regarding money.

3. What new relationship do you want to establish with your finances? For example, if you experienced your finances from a place of anxiety, do you want to change to experiencing them from gratefulness and inner peace?

4. What is one action you could take today that would start the flow of energy toward your desired relationship? When you take action to clear any part of your financial relationship, you will feel a release in the power your finances have held over you, and a freedom to create a new reality.

CARROL'S STORY

When I did this exercise, I was astounded by all the money that was flowing out in hidden costs. I was paying for several online services that I never used and had forgotten about. I realized that my inattentiveness to things like taking a television cable box back was costing me a monthly charge. As I shone my soul flashlight on each financial element, I felt more and more empowered and confident not only about taking charge of my finances but also about my life. As a result, my self-esteem improved dramatically.

For me this experience had powerful and far-reaching implications. From a position of paying minimal attention to my financial dealings and feeling immobilized and panicked about money, I realized that I could change my financial experience to one of joy and freedom. Every step I took in reclaiming my power over my finances helped me to feel more self-confident and enthusiastic. I experienced a joy and effervescence in my spirit by paying bills on time and allocating appropriate funding so there was never a financial crisis.

Remember that your financial situation is not a statement of "who you are" but instead is a reflection of learned habits and stories. If you feel constriction and stress with the subject of money, then you're not in harmony with the way you truly wish to act. As you balance the fifth chakra and speak your truth, you will discover your power to overcome seemingly overwhelming debt and feel the empowerment of owning your own financial well-being.

The Sixth Chakra: Clearing Limitations

The sixth chakra is located at the brow point, and is often called the third eye. This chakra represents your ability to open up to nonphysical realities. When it is balanced, you rely on your intuition to make decisions. When it is out of balance, you doubt every decision, looking for more information to validate your choices but often creating inner confusion.

On the physical level, the sixth chakra impacts mainly the pituitary gland, which plays an important role in the secretion and storage of endocrine hormones; these, in turn, impact the health of the whole body. On the emotional and spiritual level, the sixth chakra allows you to open up to new possibilities and trust your inner guidance. On the mental level, this chakra allows you to break through any preconceived ideas and self-defeating habits.

The following exercise will help you to strengthen your sixth chakra:

✧ Claim It! Clear and Energize Your Sixth Chakra ✧

1. Sit in a comfortable position. Look straight up and then make a full circle with your eyes, looking far to the right, down, to the left, and back to where you began. Then do a circle in the opposite direction.

2. Repeat the exercise for a minute or so.

3. Finally, relax your eyes and breathe in deeply. As you inhale through the nose, visualize the color indigo purple (the color of the sixth chakra) and hold the breath in. Let the color expand throughout your whole body, and then exhale forcefully through the mouth.

4. Repeat the breath three times.

How often have you spent your energy concentrating on what you cannot do instead of what you can do? Do you find yourself responding to an idea with all the reasons why it can't work? Are you defeating yourself by looking only at what you see as your obstacles?

Realize how much you restrict yourself when you focus on your limitations rather than on your potential. The linear mind is a master at creating reasons why things are not possible. These rationalizations are often merely a ploy to cover your fears and uncertainty. The sixth chakra doesn't rely on logic and linear thinking, but instead utilizes the power of belief, dreams, and inner guidance. To fully utilize the sixth chakra, it's helpful to clear your mind of preconceived messages and inner voices. The next exercise will help you to do that.

⸰⟨ Claim It! Quiet your Inner Voices ⟩⸰

1. Find a quiet place, preferably outside in nature.

2. Look for four rocks, and place them around you in a circle.

3. As you look at each rock separately, assign to each one a voice that you've heard inside your head that limits you. This may be something like: *You're not smart enough to do that, You can't make it happen because . . . , You can't be successful; the world is a tough place,* and so forth.

4. It may be helpful to write each statement on a piece of paper and tuck it under its rock.

5. After you've assigned each of the four rocks a voice, let the voices begin yelling their sentences at you. Experience how uncomfortable that feels.

6. Now, walk outside the circle. Step aside a few feet and see how the impact of these voices is lessened. In fact, from that new vantage point some of the phrases seem quite ridiculous.

7. Walk around the whole circle, realizing how little power each of these voices has when you don't allow them to affect you, when you separate yourself from them.

8. Now, walk back into the circle and hear the voices at their loudest level. Firmly command the voices to stop.

9. In the silence, throw each rock away and release the connection.

Each of these voices had an original intent of protecting you or in some way assisting you. They became limiting when you accepted them as being your truth. Now you realize that these phrases are just voices, not representations of reality.

Revisit this exercise when you are going through major transitions, contemplating changes, or experiencing difficulties. No matter how much discomfort, fear, and anxiety you may experience, you always have the ability to throw the rocks away and proceed without their interference and limitations.

Now that you have identified limiting voices that you have held on to and reacted to, continue clearing. What do you do in your life that reinforces the opinion of these voices? How are you allowing them to become a reality? Chloe's story is a familiar one:

> Chloe always heard an internal message that said she didn't have enough money. When she was at a friend's house and saw new furniture and new towels, she would hear her internal voice saying, *I can't afford things like that.* So, she never bought anything like that for herself and always felt, "less than."
>
> Through personal clearing work and coaching, Chloe learned to toss that belief. She opened her eyes, decided to dive into her financial reality, and saw that her poverty was just inside her. It wasn't the cost of the new towels that was holding her back; it was her belief that there wasn't enough to support what she wanted.

Remember that you have the ability to break old thought patterns that don't serve you. Be willing to recognize your limiting voices and detach from them. Utilize the power of your sixth chakra to see from the vision of the third eye, a vision that goes beyond restriction.

Seventh Chakra: Gateway to Abundance

The seventh chakra is often called the crown chakra and is located at the top of the head. This chakra represents your connection to the unknown, God, or however you interpret your higher power. When the seventh chakra is in balance, you experience a sense of connectedness and inner peace. When the seventh chakra is out of balance, you experience isolation, despair, and confusion regarding your purpose and the meaning in your life.

On the physical level, the seventh chakra affects mainly the pineal gland, impacting your ability to sleep and your daily biorhythms. On the mental level, this chakra affects your ability to stay neutral and serene, detached rather than reactive. On the emotional and spiritual levels, the seventh chakra corresponds to trust, acceptance, and the willingness to grow from any experience. The seventh chakra offers a place of relaxed and acute awareness, clearing the way to allowing manifestation to flourish. To experience that state of being, practice the following exercise:

⋰ Claim It! Clear and Energize Your Seventh Chakra ⋱

1. In a seated position, raise your arms above your head, with one hand on top of the other and making an "O" shape with your arms.

2. Inhale through the nose and hold the breath in as you visualize a white-gold color (the color of the seventh chakra), expanding through your whole body and extending outward.

3. After a few seconds, exhale forcefully through the mouth.

4. Repeat the sequence two more times. Feel the expansion of your energy field.

The seventh chakra is your window to unlimited possibilities and abundance. A key element to receive the gifts of this chakra is to have faith and let go of the need to understand or figure out every step along the way.

This is the chakra that is most closely connected to your spiritual self. Access to it is most readily found in quiet moments of meditation rather than in the fervor of everyday business. It is often in the stillness of contemplation that you can expand and open up to the guidance of your spirit. One of the ways to prepare yourself to be able to experience the wisdom of the seventh chakra is to focus your attention on what you are grateful for. Allow this gratitude to encompass your whole body on every level: physical, emotional, mental, heart, and spiritual. Then anchor it into your consciousness to serve as a pathway to your seventh chakra.

CARROL'S STORY

I remember a period in my life when I was preoccupied with a specific worry about my daughter. I was on a hike with my husband in the gorgeous mountains of Arizona. Suddenly I looked up at a craggy mountain outcrop and realized I had missed all the beauty that surrounded me on the hike. This revelation astounded me, and as I looked at the breathtaking mountain peak, I repeated to myself over and over, "I am grateful for this. I choose to store this."

My focus immediately changed. As I repeated the mantra, I was able to clear my mind and my heart of the burden I had been carrying, and I was able to truly experience the beauty around me. I immediately felt better. Later, when the problem was resolved, I could still see each of the pictures I had stored in my mind, as clear as the moment I'd first seen them.

You can use the same approach in your life. As you see or experience something that fills you with joy, repeat the phrase, "I am grateful for this. I choose to store this." Much like a bank account, those images and experiences you put into your mind's "savings account" can be drawn out and used at any time for an immediate positive refocusing of your energy and connection to your spiritual self.

The more you do this exercise, the more you will be able to appreciate different aspects of your life. In fact, you can actually expect that wonderful things will be in your path. The following exercise will help you develop this expression of abundance.

⚡ Claim It! One Gift a Day ⚡

1. Every morning, set your intention to receive the gift of opportunity. Believe that this gift will come to you, and ask your seventh chakra to help you recognize it. Don't think in a linear manner about what the gift may be, or try to orchestrate it to be something you want. You are opening up to possibilities that are beyond your conscious thought. All you have to do is pay attention.

2. At the end of the day, think back and realize what your gift was. You may even discover that you received more than one gift. What will you do with this gift? What does it open up for you? What does it help you learn? How can you take advantage of what you've received?

By deepening your practice of gratitude, you develop the ability to receive while staying present and grounded. This allows you to strengthen your spiritual self and be open to the mysteries of the Universe, welcoming messages beyond logic and reason.

You've explored many ways to clarify your thoughts and intentions, to heal yourself, and to use the power of your seven chakras to integrate the wisdom of your whole body and spirit. This invites authentic manifestation to occur in harmony with your true essence.

You've realized that the magic lies within you. Now is the time to design your life in a manner that supports your continued growth. In the next chapter, we'll help you integrate all your learning and, by using your inner guidance, create a life balance that supports your manifestation moment to moment.

Your Inner Guidance Knows the Path to Creating Life Balance

Throughout this book you've had the opportunity to develop your personal awareness of your deepest desires and your soul mission as well as your self-imposed limitations. You've learned that when your decisions and actions are in harmony with your essence, you are more able to manifest your true desires. Now is the time to create life balance.

When you are in balance, you are relaxed, open, and able to listen to the many opportunities available to you moment to moment. You are at your best, vibrant and confident in your power to manifest the life you truly want.

In this chapter we'll explore two ways to develop your internal guidance system to create balance. The first focuses on integrating and utilizing the information available to you using the chakra system, discussed in the last chapter. The second teaches you how to use the wisdom of the five elements: earth, water, fire, air, and ether.

With all the personal work you're doing, more and more options will become available to you. As exciting as this is, too many possibilities may at times make you feel overwhelmed, generating confusion and even paralysis. You may not know how to proceed or which new paths to take advantage of. Once again, the answer lies within you.

The Wisdom of Your Chakras

The chakra system is a powerful tool in helping you make decisions. By accessing the inner knowing available through each chakra, you will gain invaluable information beyond logic and reason to assist in your decision-making process for all parts of your life. Below is a process for self-discovery developed by Dr. Ann Marie Chiasson, faculty member of the Arizona Center for Integrative Medicine with Dr. Andrew Weil. Use this exercise to discover for yourself the powerful insights that each chakra has to offer.

⤳ Claim It! The Answer from Within ⤳

Think of a question you need an answer to. Choose something that is important to you. Perhaps you've vacillated with this problem, considering many options. Instead of pondering further using your logic and your intellect, go to your body and your chakra system for clarification.

Here are some examples of questions you might ask:

- *Should I move or stay where I am?*

- *Should I invest or should I not?*

- *Is this person telling me the truth? Should I trust him or her?*

- *Do I really want to enroll in this program of study?*

As you ask your specific question, solicit the wisdom of each chakra, observing the answer you get on each level. You will be amazed by the clarity that comes from this process.

Here are the steps:

1. Using seven pieces of paper, cut out seven large circles (one circle from each piece). Number each circle one through seven so that each corresponds to a chakra. Then place the seven circles in a line on the floor approximately two feet apart.

2. Stand on circle number one. Concentrate on your first chakra and contemplate your question.

3. Pay attention to your experience. Notice if there is excitement, fear, energy, constriction, acceptance, joy, and so on. This is not a yes or no answer. You're observing your experience from the viewpoint of that chakra.

4. Move to the next circle and repeat the same process from the vantage point of the second chakra.

5. Continue this process through all seven chakras.

6. At the end of the process, write in your journal the information you have received, utilizing the wisdom you learned from each chakra. Most of the time, you will have the clarity you were searching for.

Let's look at what happened to Ben, one of our clients. Ben was a very powerful financial VP in a large corporation who had just been offered the position of CEO. Despite the attractive offer, he wasn't sure if that was the right move for him. We invited Ben to answer his own question guided by the wisdom of his chakras.

When he accessed his first chakra, he realized that he wasn't grounded or present. As he moved to his second chakra, he experienced mixed feelings, including excitement and fear. At the third chakra, he felt confident that he could do the job well. As he accessed his fourth chakra, he experienced a feeling of isolation but no other emotions or sensations. At the fifth chakra, he realized he was afraid of hurting people by some of the things he would need to say in order to do his job. At the sixth chakra, he again experienced conflicting thoughts and emotions and felt almost dizzy. When he accessed the seventh chakra, he felt nothing uplifting, which surprised him since the job offer sounded so inviting.

The messages Ben received from his chakras helped him clarify his decision. Particularly significant to him was that the heart (fourth) chakra and the spiritual (seventh) chakra did not associate any joy or fulfillment with the job offer. He decided not to accept the promotion and to instead look for another opportunity that would serve him better. He opted for a smaller organization with a stronger sense of community, where he has been both successful and much happier.

Ben's story proves that when you honor your essence and listen to your inner knowing without preconceived ideas, you're able to create the balance necessary to manifest the life you desire. The knowledge of the chakra system is always available to you, and the more you access the messages of your chakras, the more you will learn to rely on that inner knowing.

Finding Life Balance Using the Five Elements

Another important approach to life balance that can be extremely beneficial is examining how you integrate and experience the five elements: earth, water, fire, air, and ether. Like the chakra system, the concept of the five elements gives you insights that do not come from your logical mind but from your energy field. Each element holds a range of unique qualities that are part of your personality, and as you discover your unique combination of these elements, you are able to better understand yourself and achieve balance at a deeper level.

Many spiritual traditions emphasize the importance of the five elements. In Japanese philosophy, Hinduism, Buddhism, and in the Chinese and Tibetan traditions, these five elements have been used for medicine, spiritual balance, and well-being. And while not all of the five elements are represented the same way in each tradition, in many they overlap.

According to the yogic tradition, you are made of five primary qualities, elements, or vibrations called *tattvas*. These elements are earth, water, fire, air, and ether; and your personality depends on which element is predominant in your life.

First, let's discover the principal qualities of each of the five elements.

The Earth Element

The core qualities of the earth element are stability and reliability, common sense and predictability. The pace of life is slow. The earth has clear boundaries.

If you don't have enough earth element, you lack security in many areas of your life and you will avoid taking risks. Whether you are aware of it or not, you are creating your life to avoid danger or failures. You have a tendency to underestimate who you are, and as a result your ability to manifest in life is very limited.

If, on the other hand, you have too much earth element, you believe that the answer to success is working harder. You lose sight of the big picture and get stuck focusing on the processes, rules, or structures to create results. There is no room for the unexpected. Your challenge in life is to trust and be detached from the "how" to get everything done. You believe that in order to manifest, you need to know everything before you can begin anything.

When the earth element is balanced in your life, you are solid, loyal, reliable, predictable, and need time to process information. You feel the need for a generous amount of information before making a decision, and change does not happen easily, yet deep inside you have the potential to accept and embrace any situation.

The Water Element

The core qualities of the water element are flow, playfulness, and connection. The pace of life is a little faster than the earth element.

If you don't have enough water element in your life, you tend to isolate yourself and disconnect from what you enjoy in life. Your life may be "under control," yet you don't connect to your joy. Life becomes merely a series of events that gives you a sense of emptiness.

If you have too much water element, you become a compulsive people pleaser, inconsistent in your behavior and at times moody. You believe that in order to manifest with success, you need to predict what other people need and act upon it. When this happens, you disconnect from your own needs and become easily depleted. Your challenge in life is to truly listen to yourself and others and let go of what others may think.

When the water element is balanced in your life, you're playful and flexible. You love reaching out and communicating with others. Harmony is important for you, and deep inside, you have the potential to rejuvenate and take care of yourself.

The Fire Element

The core qualities of the fire element are authenticity, purity, passion, courage, commitment, and invincibility.

If you don't have enough fire element, you become extremely self-centered and insecure. You spend a lot of time comparing yourself to others, and your ability to speak your truth is very limited. You believe that manifestation happens purely by luck.

If you have too much fire element, you become reactive and see the world around you as black or white, without any shades of gray. You may carry too much negativity and your style of communication may be too direct, holding at times too much anger. You feel a sense of justice and believe that the manifestation process should be fair. You shut down when things don't go your way. Your challenge in life is tolerance and acceptance of your vulnerability.

When the fire element is in balance in your life, you are authentic, courageous, passionate, and engaged in your actions. Community (family, friends, organizations) is very important to you. You love to support causes and create justice around you. The strengths you carry inside are your compassion and your ability to let go.

The Air Element

The core qualities of the air element are speed, existing without boundaries, and the ability to shift gears very quickly.

If you don't have enough air element in your life, you criticize any new ways of approaching a situation. You are allergic to change. There is always a good reason why you cannot do something. Your way is the only way to do things, and you feel that you always know best.

If you have too much air element, you say yes to too many projects without taking the time to assess how long it will take to do them all. In fact, you aren't interested in thinking about the implementation before saying yes to a project because you believe everything is possible. Even when you are depleted, you continue running and become engaged in too many things. Your manifestation principle is "certainly I can," even if the goal isn't realistic. Your challenge in life is to avoid overcommitting and to listen to what your physical body needs.

When the air element is balanced in your life, you are quick to respond and have an open mind. You see opportunities everywhere. You are creative and think outside the box; nothing can limit you. Your optimism is contagious. You have the ability to constantly uplift others.

The Ether Element

The core qualities of the ether element are stillness, acceptance of the unknown, quiet presence, and belief in infinite possibilities.

If you don't have enough ether element in your life, your motto is "I will believe it when I see it," and you don't like to anticipate positive outcomes. You lose your belief in miracles. You reject any idealism, yet deep inside you know that something is missing.

If you have too much ether element, you shift from being spacious with others to being spacey. You undervalue the physical reality, and you most likely have challenges manifesting. You think that your spirit is the only catalyst for success on Earth and are reticent to take action. You believe that making choices limits your possibilities, and you would rather dream your life than live your dreams.

When the ether element is in balance in your life, you are intuitive and open. You are able to energetically support others. You listen to people without having a hidden agenda, and you are at peace with yourself and the world. You feel serene and grateful. You have a real strength in being able to trust the unknown and follow your soul longing.

Every human being has all five elements, and it is important for your optimal manifestation for all the elements to be in constant balance and harmony. Now it's time to assess your relationship with the five elements and understand how they operate in your life, both when you manifest with great success and when you get stuck. The following exercise will help you to assess how the five elements are represented within you:

◄ Claim It! Assess Your Five Elements ►

1. Pick a situation where you're not manifesting what you want.

2. Assess yourself in that situation from the vantage point of the elements. Is each element balanced within you? You may discover that some of the elements may be very strong and others less so. This can vary according to what the situation is and how you relate to it. The following charts will help you evaluate this.

EARTH		
Balanced	**Too Much**	**Not Enough**
Stable	Rigid	Insecure
Reliable	Base decisions solely on facts, not on intuition	Don't take risks
Secure	Feel comfortable only when everything is planned and predictable	Undervalue yourself
Have common sense		
Take time to make decisions		

167

WATER		
Balanced	**Too Much**	**Not Enough**
Playful	Have compulsive behaviors	Disconnect from others
Flexible	A pleaser; what people think is more important than your personal needs	Lack joy and pleasure
Create harmony		Have too much willpower
Self-nurturing		
Spontaneous		

FIRE		
Balanced	**Too Much**	**Not Enough**
Authentic	Reactive	Self-centered
Courageous	Lack nuance	Comparing
Passionate	Judgmental	Manipulating
Engaged/ committed	Use abrupt communication	Lack truth-telling
Use direct communication		Lack trust
Have trust		
Have a sense of community		

AIR		
Balanced	**Too Much**	**Not Enough**
Open-minded	Overcommit/ under-deliver	Have a negative attitude
Quick	Lack boundaries	Resistant to change
See opportunities	Lack self-care	Not open to new ideas
Creative		
Uplift from the heart		
Believe everything is possible		

ETHER		
Balanced	**Too Much**	**Not Enough**
Intuitive	Spacey/not grounded	Not open to the mystery of life
Receptive	Lack follow-through	Need everything to be logical
Transparent/lack hidden agenda	Have difficulty making choices	Don't believe in miracles
Have inner peace	Dream instead of take action	
Aligned with your soul mission		
Always connected to receive guidance		
Fulfilled		

3. Write in your journal your assessment of each of the elements in the context of the situation you are examining. Which elements are too weak, and which elements are too strong?

4. By viewing this assessment, decide which element you would like to focus on to create more balance in your life. What actions might you take to help promote that? Here are some examples of questions to ask yourself about each element that will help you get in touch with and balance the five elements in your life:

- **Earth:** *Do I feel grounded and secure? Can I see the big picture? Am I confident in my decisions?*

- **Water:** *What brings me joy? Is my life nurturing, and do I choose things that serve me? Do I connect well with people, and can I share who I am?*

- **Fire:** *Am I authentic and understanding, or am I reactive and judgmental? Can I forgive? Can I be vulnerable? Can I be supported?*

- **Air:** *Am I able to see creative solutions and think "outside the box"? Can I serve myself first? Can I set boundaries? Does it please me to uplift others?*

- **Ether:** *Can I trust and take action without knowing the answer? Am I in touch with my spiritual self? Do I empower my intuition?*

5. In your journal, write what you've discovered about your relationship with your five elements. By seeing where there are weaknesses and strengths, you may want to take specific action to balance the elements most out of balance.

Let's look at how Emilie used this exercise to better understand the challenges she was facing regarding a lack of happiness in her life:

Emilie had experienced a comfortable childhood and seemed outwardly pleased with her life. Everything seemed to be working around her. She had a successful career and a lifestyle that matched her needs. Emilie was a loyal and reliable person, dedicated to serving those in her community. She found great joy in the happiness of others. She was very practical, quick, and great at solving people's problems.

At the age of 55, she attended a workshop of ours on exploring one's soul mission. During the seminar, Emilie burst into tears as she realized that she had been burying a feeling of emptiness deep inside for many years.

How can we assess Emilie? Below is what she discovered about herself from the viewpoint of her five elements.

- The earth element is strong in Emilie: She is loyal, pragmatic, and reliable.

- The water element is lacking. Despite a pleasant lifestyle, she misses authentic connection with others, and she doesn't have enough joy. She realizes that she cannot access her true happiness if people around her are not happy.

- The fire element is in balance. She loves to be part of various communities serving others, and volunteers regularly. She gets energized when she does this.

- The air element is depleted. Despite the fact that she is quick to jump into new opportunities, she often falls into a routine that doesn't uplift her.

- The ether element is strongly lacking. Emilie is not fulfilled; she doesn't feel she has a purpose, despite the many things that are working well in her life.

After discovering through examining the five elements what was going on for her, Emilie decided to develop the water element *(How can I have more joy in my life, and how can I feel more connected?)* and the ether element *(What is my life purpose?)*. Today Emilie is taking a sailing class to bring her more joy and has taken a trip to Bali with some friends to explore that country's spiritual heritage.

As you have seen in other parts of this book, important insights sometimes come when we view ourselves with different lenses. An excellent way to facilitate balance with your five elements is through the visualization process. Images often speak louder than words, and they will help you make the necessary changes for your desired manifestation.

⋰ Claim It! Journey to Your Five Elements ⋱

1. Close your eyes and think of a time when your manifestation process has been extremely successful.

2. Notice how each element appears in your visualization. For example:

- For the earth element, do you see a vast mountain, a forest, or a Zen garden?

- Is the water element represented by an ocean, a lake, a river, or drops of rain?

- Does the fire element look like a campfire, a fireplace, the flame of a candle, or a torch?

- Does the air element resemble a soft breeze blowing leaves on a tree, a crisp cold air, or pure stillness?

- Is the ether element represented by intense light, a specific color, or the vastness of outer space?

3. Now that you have images for each element, find representations of these in magazines, calendars, or on the Internet.

4. Assemble these images into a collage on a piece of poster board.

5. Place this collage where you'll frequently see it, reminding yourself of your ideal balance of the five elements to facilitate manifestation.

In this chapter, you've placed into your manifesting toolbox two more invaluable tools. In the next chapter, you'll learn the importance of incorporating into your day-to-day life these and the many other tools you have discovered that help you connect to your true essence. This is necessary to keep the magical unfolding happening as you experience fulfillment and manifestation moment to moment.

CONCLUSION

Infinite Possibilities Exist Within

As you reach the end of this book, you must prepare to incorporate your new wisdom into your daily life. This chapter presents an implementation plan that will carry you forward: 1) An everyday practice to keep your soul toned and in tune with its mission; 2) Some cues for dealing with the inevitable blocks that will appear in your path; and 3) A manifestation backpack carrying the tools you need to turn what you've learned into elements of success.

The success of your ability to manifest lies within you, moment to moment, every day of your life. Carl Jung, Swiss psychiatrist and founder of Analytical Psychology, said, "Your vision will become clear only when you can look into your heart. Who looks outside, dreams; who looks inside, awakes." You alone design your path; you alone reap the benefits of self-discovery and the reframing of your reality. Awakening your intuition, discovering your soul mission, and getting rid of the baggage that is holding you down must all be done from the inside out. This journey will open up for you a world of infinite possibilities.

Finding a Daily Spiritual Practice

Many spiritual teachers have said that meditation is your first step toward happiness, and almost every spiritual tradition emphasizes the importance of daily practice. This daily practice can take many forms: for some religions, a silent meditation is done staring at a picture of a holy person or a mandala. Often the reading of scripture or a mantra is used as a daily practice. Many of the breath exercises we've included in this book can be used as a daily practice. Walking meditations and even dancing can serve as a daily practice.

There are many options to look at as you find a daily practice that resonates with you. Some teachers recommend doing your practice several times a day, at a specific time of the day, and/or for a specific period of time. In the end, everyone agrees that spiritual practice needs to be embraced at least daily. Your practice doesn't need to take a lot of time or money. You don't need the right clothes, the right books, the right altar, or the right guru. The only requirements are you and your commitment.

Understanding how you respond to commitment is important. How do you experience commitment? Does it create a feeling in you of inner pressure and rigidity? If so, does this internal pressure help you to stay on track, or does it make you feel trapped? What do you do when you experience a setback or don't fulfill your commitments? How do you judge yourself then, positively or negatively?

Committing to Self

Commitment is often perceived as an added duty and responsibility, something more to add to your already busy life. As you contemplate committing to a daily practice, you may experience some of the following reactions: you feel trapped, you wonder if you are making the right commitment, you fear you will have less time for fun and pleasure. Despite this reticence, we invite you to look at the concept of commitment from a new perspective.

There are four major benefits associated with the process of commitment.

1. Commitment gives you authentic freedom. When you commit, your mind isn't wondering if what you are doing is the right thing; you are engaged moment to moment and not questioning if you should be in or out of your commitment.

2. Commitment helps you to achieve what you want. Every performer and athlete reaches their mastery through the consistency and quality of their commitment. Their talent and desire alone will never be enough to achieve their goals.

3. Commitment is the highway to growth. It brings you constant feedback. Whether you are committing to a relationship or you commit to a performance, you will experience reality checks on a regular basis that will help you be aware of your limitations and your potential.

4. Commitment helps you create a high level of integrity in your life. When your words match your actions, you're not just energetically dragging along all the projects you said you were going to do. Your life force is much stronger and much clearer when you take action on a regular basis, allowing you to attract what you truly want.

Working on your ability to make a commitment is one of the most effective ways to manifest the changes you desire for yourself. The way you behave toward the commitment you have made to your spiritual practice is the way you will behave toward all endeavors and responsibilities in life, which will have a major impact on what you are able to manifest. As you keep honoring your personal commitments by engaging in them day after day, you will be evolving and realigning many parts of your life, thus creating self-mastery and manifestation that is aligned at the highest level—with your soul.

TEJPAL'S STORY

For a long time I searched for a spiritual practice that resonated with me. When I was 16 years old, I wanted to be a perfect yogi, able to experience bliss and true happiness. I thought that through my will and with discipline, I would be able to manifest what my soul longed for.

At that time, I started a daily practice but dropped it after a few weeks when I didn't experience instant rewards. Later in my life, I continued my search and tried different kinds of yoga, Qi Gong, and various Buddhist practices. Each of these attempts at a daily spiritual practice lasted about six to nine months. Finally, when I discovered Kundalini yoga, the fit was instantaneous.

After ten minutes of my first Kundalini yoga class, I said, "Thank you, I really found home." I set the intent to start a daily practice but was amazed by the amount of pressure I was putting on myself to keep this commitment. As I struggled with this, I saw how that internal stress was a pattern that appeared with every commitment I had ever created in my life. Upon making that realization, I set the intent to release unnecessary stress and do my practice out of a sense of joy and for what it offered me. Through honoring my commitment to the daily practice of Kundalini yoga, I learned how to approach commitment from a new, relaxed, yet focused place, without inner constriction and tension.

I started to allow more flow in my life and shifted from being driven and combative to being open and more receptive to opportunities. My new behavior started to show up in my relationship with food and the rigidity of my workout regimens. For many years, my desire and commitment to stay fit had created anxiety in my life. My spiritual practice taught me to be more relaxed and to realize that keeping a commitment didn't require such rigid behaviors. I chose to get rid of my scale, trusting my ability to keep my intent without stressing, and discovered the true joy of challenging myself physically while adapting easily to life circumstances.

Over the years there have been only a few times when I've neglected my spiritual practice. One time comes to mind and still makes me smile. During an advanced Kundalini yoga teacher-training course, I was assigned to do a certain meditation for 90 days in a row. It involved a 31-minute daily practice, which I did every morning, although I wasn't fond of the meditation chosen for me. On the morning of day 89, I realized that I had forgotten to do the meditation the previous day. That meant I had to start all over again at day 1. Realizing what I had done, I felt devastated and considered not honoring the commitment thoroughly. Then I remembered that I was a teacher, and being true to self was deeply connected to my soul purpose. Chagrined, I started my meditation practice again, letting go of my self-recriminations and surrendering to the process.

Many people want to have a daily spiritual practice, and yet few actually follow through and establish a regular regimen. In some ways, choosing a spiritual practice is like choosing a diet . . . which one will work for you? Which is the best? As with everything, the answer lies within you.

Trust Your Body

The way to select a spiritual practice is not through your mind, not because someone told you to, and not because another person received great benefits from it. Make your decision based upon your own physical experiences. Listen to your body. Does the meditation or tradition you're trying out bring you pleasure, peace, strength, or serenity? If not, try something else until you find what does.

As you seek out options to explore, your intuition will guide you. Notice what presents itself to you. This inspiration may appear as happenstance. For example, you are on a plane and in the seat next to you is a person who is involved in a spiritual path and tells you there is a gathering in the hotel next to where you will be staying. Or it may be a book that catches your eye, or a casual conversation with a friend that stirs a longing inside you. You may walk into a restaurant and see a group of people who just came from a yoga class you've been curious about. Whatever shows up, if it sparks your interest or stirs you in some way, explore it!

Just Show Up!

No matter how long you have done your practice, there will be days when you feel centered and others when you feel scattered. There will be times you experience great benefits from your practice and other times you show up and appear to get nothing out of it. And there may even be times you can't wait for your practice to be done. It's all part of learning commitment, and it's all worthwhile. No matter what, just continue to show up! Let your practice do its own work and it will transform you, just as it did Tejpal.

So What to Do?

As we've mentioned, all of the breath exercises in this book are options for a daily practice. Pick one that particularly appeals to you, or select something else that attracts you. Set a reasonable amount of time for your daily practice, perhaps 3 to 15 minutes per day. Decide a time of the day that works best for you, and establish a place in your home that you can designate as a sacred space. Set your intent to commit for 40 days in a row, since it takes 40 days to create a habit.

The following exercise is another option for a daily practice. It was originally created by Carrol to assist performers in clearing their minds and establishing focus before important concerts and presentations. It will help you to experience clarity and energy, and to reboot your system. In addition to being an option for a daily practice, anyone can use this exercise at any point in the day as a powerful way to realign their energy.

❧ Claim It! Five-Point Readiness ❧

1. *Grounding:* Stand with your feet hip-width apart. Point your toes slightly inward. Imagine that roots, like the roots of a tree, are going down from the bottom of your feet, far into the ground. From deep inside the earth, the energy rises up through those roots and into you as you ground and connect. You might imagine the energy like a pyramid with the widest part of the pyramid lodged deep in the earth and the tip of the pyramid rising up to rest at your heart center, your fourth chakra.[1]

2. *Tuning in:* Pull your tailbone under and tuck it in. This elongates the spine and forces the shoulders back. Pull in the navel and lower abdomen, accessing all the energy of the lower triangle or pyramid of your body. From this position of power, recall a time when you were outstanding. It might have been when you received an award or gave a particularly successful presentation. It might be when someone you valued gave you a compliment. Think about that time, re-experiencing it with all your senses. How did it feel? Where were you? What were you wearing? Can you recall all the details about that event? Make it as real as you can, and experience again how great it made you feel. Hold that feeling a moment, and then take a deep breath and relax while still keeping the sensation of how empowered you felt. This "Circle of Excellence" is yours to experience whenever you need an energy realignment.[2]

3. *One-minute breath:* While still standing, inhale slowly through your nose for a count of 5, with approximately one count per second. Hold the breath in for a count of 5. Then exhale slowly through your nose for a count of 5. Repeat this a number of times as you build up the duration on each of the three steps: inhale, hold, and exhale. You can increase gradually to 7 counts, 9 counts, and so on, each time; or you can jump to 10 or 15 counts and build up from there. Aim at the ideal of 20 counts, which means you complete one full breath in a minute. Do this for two to three minutes. You will feel your energy shift dramatically to a calm and clear state of being.[3]

4. *Reset your brain:* Raise both arms out to the side, with palms facing up and the fingers of each hand forming a claw. Keep tension in your fingers as you raise your arms to cross above your head, allowing the arms to bend, and then back down. Do this first with the right hand crossing in front and then the left. Breathe in through your nose each time your arms go up, exhale as they come down. Repeat for two to three minutes. This Kundalini yoga "Lion's Paws" exercise rewires the brain for clarity and focus. Pressure in the hand reconnects each lobe of the brain and balances your energy. Crossing the arms above the head reconnects the left brain (linear/logical mind) and the right brain (intuitive/creative mind).[4]

5. *Access visual mode:* Look up and *envision success!* When you raise your eyes, you put yourself into Visual mode. In your mind's eye, visualize yourself confident and full of joy and enthusiasm as you surmount all challenges. Being in Visual also negates fear and helps you overcome difficulties.

You've seen the importance and value of committing to a daily practice. As you get further into your practice, you'll discover many benefits of this discipline. Carrol has also done Kundalini yoga regularly; including periods of not honoring her commitment, she's had it as a daily practice for more than 20 years. Here is her experience:

CARROL'S STORY

When I do Kundalini yoga in the morning, my day flows in a much more seamless way. I feel an inner calmness that allows me to work through problems without becoming reactive or embroiled in confusion. On those days that I skip my morning practice, it's as if I'm going out into the world without my spiritual shield to buffer me from the stresses I encounter.

Even when you are consistent in honoring your daily spiritual practice, you will inevitably still experience times of feeling stuck or out of alignment. As we'll discuss next, these obstacles can become one of your greatest assets.

The Value Behind Your Blocks

All of us have experienced feeling stuck, confused, or challenged by what seems insurmountable in our life. When this happens, depending on your life experience, you may go into a mind-set of frustration, lack of hope and energy, and perhaps even blame. You may start to build up negativity and judgment toward yourself and wonder how you ended up in that situation and what part is truly your responsibility. As you do this, you reinforce being stuck and go deeper into the situation you are trying desperately to remove yourself from.

These self-sabotaging and unintentional actions and thought patterns make up your personal blocks. We are trained to view our blocks as negative, inhibiting growth and potential. However, when you choose to look at these blocks as a growth opportunity, your ability to manifest expands exponentially. Most of the time, your blocks in life are an invitation for you to look at aspects of you that are disconnected from your true self. Your blocks are often the mirror of what is going on inside of you. They come from within.

The problem is never the block itself, but rather how you handle it. Too often, you're dismissing the true nature of what's going on and focusing on how you "should" react, perhaps feeling inadequate for the task at hand. As the Spiritual Psychology program at the University of Santa Monica in California states: "How you deal with the issue *is* the issue."[5]

See if you can identify the blocks in the following examples:

Sylvia has been an expert in her field for many years and is well recognized and respected. As the years went by, she lost interest in her work and little by little was unable to honor her commitments. She knew it was time for a life change; she had no energy to perform in her previous career and yet no motivation to dive into something new. She was stuck. She became more and more judgmental with herself, not happy with her performance and her lack of action. She knew it was time to move on and make clear choices about her future, yet she always postponed taking action, causing her to feel completely exhausted. She was very aware of her avoidance mechanism but had no clue on how to move forward.

Renee is a creative and pragmatic entrepreneur. Every idea she has turns into a successful project. She is full of energy and enthusiasm. On the personal side, she is very clear about the unhealthy situation she has created in her intimate relationship. She truly knows what she should do but seems unable to do anything about it and blames herself for it. She hopes someday that she'll be able to better her personal situation, but for the time being she buries herself in expanding her business.

Rob is a great developer who takes on new projects constantly. His life is overloaded and his sleep is disrupted, yet he cannot stop the cycle. As a result, his delivery is never on time and he's completely overwhelmed. He knows he overcommits, but he can't stop the pattern.

Michelle runs her own organization, helping families who are faced with the challenges of their loved ones going through the dying process. She is never at home before 11 P.M., and her house is a mess. She hates how she lives, but she can't stop the cycle.

As you read these stories, you can begin to understand that the underlying blocks come from emotions that haven't been processed.

- Sylvia experiences tremendous fear of failure. Even at her most successful, that fear is so intense that she has no choice but to be the very best at what she does.

- Renee experiences extreme anxiety and the fear of rejection and being hurt.

- Rob experiences intense fear of not having enough and being isolated.

- Michelle is terrified to say no.

All of these emotions are real, and they truly run these people's lives. By trying to avoid dealing with our blocks, we actually allow them to take over our lives. If, instead, we express these emotions, little by little their intensity will diminish, and we'll experience our main challenges from a different perspective. We will feel empowered.

When you identify a block, your first question might be: *What should I do?* You search for guidelines with specific tools to "solve" the situation, actually ignoring the block itself, which stems from unexamined and unexpressed emotions. While there are no fast answers, the following exercise is a great approach to help you identify, deal with, and benefit from your blocks:

⋇ Claim It! All Out! ⋇

Choose a situation in life where you experience recurring challenges.

1. Instead of wondering what to do and how to handle that problem, connect to the emotions behind the issue that you are experiencing.

2. Commit to writing in your journal for five minutes a day about your experience with that particular feeling.

Do you experience fear, anxiety, terror, or panic? Can you identify the main emotion? Usually it's an emotion you're not comfortable with. In your attempt to avoid facing this emotion, you create behaviors that aren't aligned with your essence. These behaviors are merely symptoms of the underlying issue. In brief, you create a monster!

The less you want to connect to your uncomfortable emotions, the bigger and more powerful your monster becomes. The more you integrate these emotions into your life, the more you will be able to act in alignment with your essence rather than your fears.

The first time that Michelle, one of Tejpal's clients discussed in the previous paragraphs, used this process she wrote for three hours straight. She was amazed by how much better she felt after the catharsis. It was the beginning of her inner transformation, and her hope and excitement were priceless to witness. The constant terror she had felt seemed less intense. The fact that she was giving light to this hidden part of herself helped her to be more aware of the root of her behavior and allowed her to take her power back.

Destination Manifestation

You have now discovered that beneath each of your blocks is a secret trapdoor leading to a path of greater manifestation. Equally important in carrying you along that path is realizing and celebrating all that you have already accomplished. The following exercise will guide you:

⅋ Claim It! Marvel at Your Skills ⅋

Take a moment to reflect on all of the insights you've gained as you've worked through this book, the "Aha!" moments you've experienced, and the actions you've taken or intend to take. All of these important insights work together to establish the perfect scenario for you to become a masterful manifester and to achieve the life you desire. Recall each of the principles of manifestation, and use your manifesting journal to create and fill in a chart like the one on the next two pages:

Principle	My Aha Moment	Actions I Am Taking
1. You Have a Unique Soul Mission	*What I am good at doesn't bring me joy.* *My limiting behavior (being depressed) doesn't define who I am.* *It's okay to be afraid.*	*Journaling for 40 days on what brings me joy.* *At least once a day, choosing to bring hope to a person I meet.* *Practicing the tapping Claim It! Release and Renew every day.*
2. It's All About Energy	*I rely too much on my logical mind and don't listen enough to the intelligence of my body.* *When I get stuck emotionally, I know how to shift quickly.* *Resting is a tool to help me experience more joy and creativity.*	*Minimum once a week, practicing the 360-degree Claim It! to get more insights.* *Remembering to use all three modes: how it feels, how it sounds, and how it looks.* *Blocking out one day per week to rejuvenate and not do any work.*
3. Intuition Is the Magic Wand		
4. Your Belief and Your Story Do Not Define You and Can Be Changed		
5. Your Desire Forms the Basis of Every Manifestation		
6. Intention Overcomes Every Obstacle		

7. You Have the Power to Clear, Heal, and Reinvent Constantly		
8. Your Inner Guidance Knows the Path to Creating Life Balance		

Once you have completed your chart, look back at all the "Aha!" moments you've had and imagine all the parts of you that are joining together to create a new, successful platform from which to manifest. Some of these insights have been in your energy field for a long time and have occasionally "nibbled" at your consciousness to be heard and brought alive. Sometimes we know more than we give ourselves credit for. This is born out in Carrol's story.

CARROL'S STORY

Several years ago I was on the phone doing an interview for a Canadian newspaper. The interviewer asked me, "How many concerts are you doing next year?" Without hesitation, I responded, "Sixty-seven." After the telephone conversation was completed, I thought to myself, *It's funny that it was so easy for me to say 67 concerts with such authority. The year hasn't even started yet, and my concert bookings haven't begun. I wonder why I said that number?*

Then, at income tax time the following year, as I reviewed my concert agenda for the year before, I recalled the strange sensation I'd had during that phone call and checked my records to see exactly how many concerts I had played. I still recall my feeling of amazement when I discovered that I'd performed exactly 67 concerts. I had precisely manifested my intent.

Carrol trusted her intuition and inner guidance and allowed it to propel her toward manifesting her desire. You, too, have all the potential necessary to manifest your truest desires on a moment-to-moment basis. Take some time to honor and congratulate yourself on all that you have already achieved. You have dug deep inside yourself to clarify, clear, assess, and reenergize. You've focused your intent and desire to serve your soul mission. Recall for a moment your new tools, regarding:

1. *Soul Mission:* Remember the importance of honoring your essence, gifts, and life lesson.

2. *Energy:* Triple-channel your life with Visual, Auditory, and Kinesthetic. Be aware of your five levels: Physical, Emotional, Mental, Heart, and Spiritual. Live 360 Degrees!

3. *Intuition:* Recall the seven elements that help develop your intuition: Be clueless, be detached, be grounded, trust yourself, be a sponge, be playful, and be nurturing.

4. *Belief and Story:* Remember that you can choose to believe and change your story by using the kaleidoscope and exploring the roots of your belief system.

5. *Desire:* Evaluate how your desires are aligned with the five levels: Physical, Emotional, Mental, Heart, and Spiritual.

6. *Intention:* Strengthen your intention and explore where your motivation is based: Is it in pressure or passion?

7. *Heal and Clear Using the Chakras:* Examine seven areas of your life associated with the chakras: the first chakra, your physical space; the second chakra, your experience with time; the third chakra, judgment and acceptance; the fourth chakra, relationships; the fifth chakra, money; the sixth chakra, overcoming limitations; and the seventh chakra, allowing abundance in your life.

8. *Life Balance:* Get help with decision-making using the chakra system and balancing life with the five elements: earth, water, fire, air, and ether.

As you proceed further along this path of infinite possibilities, remember to take with you the insights and self-realizations that brought you to this point. Carry in your mind a backpack filled with everything that you've discovered and empowered yourself to use.

⋅⟨ Claim It! Manifestation Backpack ⟩⋅

As you pack your tools into your imaginary backpack, be selective. Keep it light and simple. Choose the tools and insights that propel your ability to manifest today. You can always return to home base, reassess what you need, and repack different tools to take with you and use another day.

To simplify packing, we suggest you use three compartments often referred to in yoga—that of your mind, body, and spirit.

1. *Mind:* What tools will you bring with you to . . .

- Clear your old stories

- Clarify your belief and your intent

- Uncover limiting thought patterns

- Explore the quality and truth of your desire

- Accept not to understand, but to trust

2. *Body:* What tools will you bring with you to . . .

- Remain aware of your energy and chakra centers

- Listen to the teachings of your body

- Access and balance your five elements

- Remember the power of the breath

- Rest, realign, and allow

3. *Spirit:* What tools will you bring with you to . . .

- Remember your gift

- Express your soul mission and life purpose

- Sustain your spiritual practice

- Trust your intuition

- Empower your joy factor

When Tejpal packed her backpack, she took:

- *In the Mind compartment:* Processing her desires through the five levels (physical, emotional, mental, heart, and spiritual) from Principle 5.

- *In the Body compartment:* Decision-making process using the chakra system from Principle 7.

- *In the Spiritual compartment:* Daily spiritual practice from Principle 8 and a daily focus on what brings her joy from Principle 1.

When Carrol packed her manifestation backpack, she took:

- *In the Mind compartment:* "Who is on your team?" exercise from Principle 4.

- *In the Body compartment:* Five-Point Readiness exercise from the Conclusion.

- *In the Spiritual compartment:* "Sa-ta-na-ma" walking meditation from Principle 3.

You are well prepared for your journey. We hope you enjoy the adventure. Remember to remain compassionate with yourself and others as you proceed with gratitude and openness. Our intent and desire is that you experience fulfillment and authentic joy as you travel along your soul-guided path to manifest moment to moment.

Pack your backpack and take off!

Claim it!

NOTES

Principle 3

1. Yogi Bhajan, *The Aquarian Teacher: KRI Level One Instructor Yoga Manual* (Kundalini Research Institute, 2005): 425.

Principle 6

1. Esther and Jerry Hicks, *Ask and It Is Given: Learning to Manifest Your Desires* (Carlsbad, CA: Hay House, 2004).

2. Yogi Bhajan, "Five Sutras for the Aquarian Age," inspired by the Indian philosopher Patanjali, from 150 B.C., *The Aquarian Teacher: Level One Instructor Textbook, 4th edition* (Santa Cruz, NM: KRI Publishing, 2007): 6.

3. Viktor E. Frankl, *Man's Search for Meaning* (Boston, MA: Beacon Press, 2006): 66.

Principle 7

1. Exercise known as "Spinal Flex" in Kundalini yoga taught by Yogi Bhajan. *The Aquarian Teacher: KRI International Kundalini Yoga Teacher Training Level I Yoga Manual - Part Nine, Sets and Meditations* 3rd edition (Santa Cruz, NM: Kundalini Research Institute, 2005).

2. Exercise known as "Spinal Flex" in Kundalini yoga taught by Yogi Bhajan. *The Aquarian Teacher: KRI International Kundalini Yoga Teacher Training Level I Yoga Manual - Part Nine, Sets and Meditations* 3rd edition (Santa Cruz, NM: Kundalini Research Institute, 2005), 320.

3. This quotation is attributed to Oscar Wilde.

4. Joe Vitale and Ihaleakala Hew Len, Ph.D., *Zero Limits: The Secret Hawaiian System for Wealth, Health, Peace, and More* (Hoboken, NJ: John Wiley & Sons, 2007).

Conclusion

1. Inspired by the Nine Gates Mystery School, California, www.ninegates.org.

2. Carrol McLaughlin, *Dr. Carrol's Power Performance* (Tucson, AZ: Integrity Ink, 2008), www.integrityink.com.

3. Yogi Bhajan, *The Aquarian Teacher: Level One Instructor Textbook, 4th edition* (Santa Cruz, NM: KRI Publishing, 2007): 91.

4. Yogi Bhajan, *The Aquarian Teacher: Level One Instructor Textbook, 4th edition* (Santa Cruz, NM: KRI Publishing, 2007): 387.

5. www.universityofsantamonica.edu

ACKNOWLEDGMENTS

Throughout this project, we've felt extraordinary support and encouragement from many people. In particular, we would like to thank:

Michael Tompkins, Chief Executive Officer, Miraval Resort & Spa, for his vision, enthusiasm, support, and belief in us.

Nancy Fyffe, for her generous gifts of time and editing. Her sharp insights and commitment to help us from the very beginning are greatly appreciated.

Brookes Nohlgren, for her editing and dedicated support, and for her gracious ability to hear us and direct us in creating a cohesive whole.

Kelly Harris, Carrol's precious daughter, for her passionate commitment to help us present our ideas with focus and precision.

Lisa Bernier and the Hay House team, for their spirit of collaboration and priceless guidance.

We are deeply grateful to all of you.

ABOUT THE AUTHORS

Tejpal was the director of an international business consultant team in Paris, France, specializing in leadership development. She holds master's degrees in both business management and psychology. Realizing that her true life purpose was to inspire and uplift, she moved to the United States and attended the Barbara Brennan School of Healing and Corporate Coach University, and became a certified Kundalini yoga teacher and teacher trainer. She is also a certified hypnotherapist.

For the past 25 years, Tejpal has given weekly life-coaching, healing, and intuitive-guidance telephone sessions to clients around the world. Today, she is a highly respected life coach, healer, intuitive, and inspirational teacher at the renowned Miraval Resort & Spa in Tucson, Arizona. Tejpal leads workshops in the U.S. and abroad on intuition, healing, soul missions, vibrant living, and personal development, helping people design the life they truly desire.

Dr. Carrol McLaughlin was born in the northernmost city of Alberta, Canada—not exactly the center for harp study! Yet at age four she decided she would become one of the world's top harpists, and has made that life wish a reality. She earned her master's degree from The Juilliard School in New York and is the first person to ever receive a doctorate in harp performance.

Carrol is an internationally renowned concert artist, having performed in virtually every major concert hall, including Russia, Hong Kong, China, Korea, Thailand, Indonesia, Egypt, Brazil, Argentina, Peru, Chile, Europe, and North and South America . . . plus 33 concert tours to Japan. She is the only person authorized to perform the music of the late movie star Harpo Marx, and she has toured the U.S. and Europe performing with Harpo's son, Bill Marx. In addition, she is a prolific composer, with over 100 commissioned compositions that are now performed in major concert halls around the world.

She has participated in movie and television recordings, including in the original *Star Wars,* and has recorded 15 internationally marketed personal and ensemble CDs and DVDs. Carrol has toured the U.S. for the most respected artist management, Columbia Artists Management, playing approximately 650 concerts, and is also the founding director of the internationally acclaimed ensemble HarpFusion, who have toured and recorded extensively and were featured at the World Expo in Shanghai, China.

Carrol is now an award-winning distinguished professor at the University of Arizona, heading one of the largest and most respected harp departments. She performs internationally as a soloist and with orchestras, and she also gives workshops and lectures throughout the world. She is the author of *Power Performance,* a performer's guidebook to using Neuro-Linguistic Programming to overcome stage fright and personal inhibitions. An expert in Neuro-Linguistic Programming, a certified Kundalini yoga teacher, and a certified hypnotherapist, Carrol is also a gifted healer and has researched the power of harp music to heal patients in the intensive-care unit following heart surgery.

Website: www.ManifestMomentToMoment.com

We hope you enjoyed this Hay House book. If you'd like to receive our online catalog featuring additional information on Hay House books and products, or if you'd like to find out more about the Hay Foundation, please contact:

Hay House, Inc., P.O. Box 5100, Carlsbad, CA 92018-5100
(760) 431-7695 or (800) 654-5126
(760) 431-6948 (fax) or (800) 650-5115 (fax)
www.hayhouse.com® • www.hayfoundation.org

Published and distributed in Australia by: Hay House Australia Pty. Ltd., 18/36 Ralph St., Alexandria NSW 2015 • *Phone:* 612-9669-4299
Fax: 612-9669-4144 • www.hayhouse.com.au

Published and distributed in the United Kingdom by: Hay House UK, Ltd., Astley House, 33 Notting Hill Gate, London W11 3JQ • *Phone:* 44-20-3675-2450
Fax: 44-20-3675-2451 • www.hayhouse.co.uk

Published and distributed in the Republic of South Africa by:
Hay House SA (Pty), Ltd., P.O. Box 990, Witkoppen 2068
Phone/Fax: 27-11-467-8904 • www.hayhouse.co.za

Published in India by: Hay House Publishers India, Muskaan Complex, Plot No. 3, B-2, Vasant Kunj, New Delhi 110 070 • *Phone:* 91-11-4176-1620
Fax: 91-11-4176-1630 • www.hayhouse.co.in

Distributed in Canada by: Raincoast Books, 2440 Viking Way, Richmond, B.C. V6V 1N2 • *Phone:* 1-800-663-5714
Fax: 1-800-565-3770 • www.raincoast.com

Take Your Soul on a Vacation

Visit www.HealYourLife.com® to regroup, recharge, and reconnect with your own magnificence. Featuring blogs, mind-body-spirit news, and life-changing wisdom from Louise Hay and friends.

Visit www.HealYourLife.com today!